# Beautiful Beginnings from the East

Barbrah Orchard

Beautiful Beginnings from the East

Copyright © 2015 Barbrah Orchard
All rights reserved. No part of this publication may be reproduced, stored in a retrieval system or transmitted in any form or by any means, electronic, mechanical, photocopying, recording or otherwise, without the prior written permission of the publisher.

The information, views, opinions and visuals expressed in this publication are solely those of the author(s) and do not reflect those of the publisher. The publisher disclaims any liabilities or responsibilities whatsoever for any damages, libel or liabilities arising directly or indirectly from the contents of this publication.

A copy of this publication can be found in the National Library of Australia.

ISBN:978-1-742845-53-1 (pbk.)

Published by Book Pal
www.bookpal.com.au

# DEDICATION

In the memory of my loving, supportive dad Mzee late Silver Mugobera Gimanga. He was my role model of wisdom. The powerful words he planted in me contributed a lot to who I am today and will be remembered for eternity.

And most of all, to Jesus Christ my Lord and Saviour, through my best friend, the Holy Spirit, together we managed to finish this project.

# ACKNOWLEDGEMENTS

To my wonderful husband Shane Orchard, who unconditionally has continued to love, support and believe in the call God put in me.

To Fruitful Mission Centre Church in Uganda, who have always encouraged, supported and allowed me to pastor them. You guys are amazing.

To Agape Church Family and Apostle Phill Spence for his knowledge and devoted support of Establishing Fruitful Mission Ministries in Australia.

To Apostle David and Dee McDonald for discovering me and their support in coming to Australia which took my ministry to the next level.

To my spiritual parents, pastors John and Jessica Wandera, who I was honoured to serve under for a number of years and through their great ministry, God allowed me to come to Australia.

To two of the most loving and supportive great leaders and friends I know, Pastors Alister and Lois Lowe of Lighthouse Care Ministries, who spent hours on editing this book and made it readable. God bless you.

And finally to my fellow fighters, the Pastors of Budadiri East, my home village. Pastors of Sironko District, Pastors of Mbale District, Pastors of Kampala and outlying Districts who are great men and women of God. These men and women have endured and pushed, Uganda to the level of where it is today in the Kingdom of God.

# CONTENTS

INTRODUCTION .................................................................. 1
1. WALKING ANTI-CLOCKWISE ............................ 3
   Obstacles of Revival .................................................. 6
   The Source .................................................................. 7
   Competition and Strife between the Leaders ........ 11
      Greed .................................................................... 12
      Pride ..................................................................... 13
      Zeal ....................................................................... 15

2. BEAUTIFUL BEGINNINGS ................................. 20
   How do we set Beautiful Beginnings? ................... 21
   The Voice of Jesus ..................................................... 26

3. BUDADIRI EAST PASTORS ................................. 30
   Why did we choose This Church? .......................... 33
      Hatred .................................................................. 36
      Division ................................................................ 39
      Greed .................................................................... 47
      Pride ..................................................................... 56
      It's Never Too Late ............................................. 65
   Mountain Timber ...................................................... 67
      Self –Seeking ....................................................... 70
   Law and Grace ........................................................... 73
   Who is Leading You to the Promised Land? ........ 76
   The Source of Money ............................................... 82
   The Fear of God ......................................................... 85
   The Blessing of Esau and the Blessing of Jacob .... 90

4. MONEY .......................................................... 97
   Casting Your Bread upon Many Waters ............. 101
      Everyone Needs Money ................................... 104
      Fighting for One Another ................................ 110
      Giving by Faith ................................................. 111
      Begging ............................................................. 114
      If You Don't do it Now Then You Will Never be Able to Help .......................................................... 120
      The cost of partnering with God ..................... 122
      Revival is in you ............................................... 127

5. REPENTANCE ..................................................... 132
   Plumbline ............................................................. 135
   Seven ..................................................................... 138

6. LORD, "WE" COME TO YOU, NOT, "I "COME TO YOU ................................................................. 141
   Sharing the Anointing .......................................... 145
   Sharing Burdens ................................................... 151
   Why a Dowry is paid ........................................... 154
   Building Churches ................................................ 156

7. THE LATTER GLORY OF THE LATTER HOUSE .............................................................................. 158
   Command Your Son to Work .............................. 161
   A Woman Fights for Her Son to Have a Second Chance at Life ...................................................... 165

8. GOD COMES AT LAST ....................................... 168
   When the Latter Gory is Present Even Our Governments Will Turn Back to God ............. 172
   Signet Ring ............................................................ 173

9. IDI AMIN STARVED PEOPLE............................ 176
   The Glory Can't Be Contained In One Place ....... 178

10. THE LATTER GLORY FROM THE EAST ....... 179
    The characteristics of the people from East: ........ 182
    Donkeys and Horses ................................................ 184

11. THE COST AND THE CHALLENGES ............ 188

12. THE VISION FOR THE BUDADIRI EAST PASTORS ................................................................ 192
    Ezekiel's Ministry and Deeper Insight ................. 194
    A Vessel .....................................................................197
    A Servant ...................................................................198
    A Friend .....................................................................199
    A Child .......................................................................199
    The Difference between a Holy Spirit Led Church and a Church That Depends on Their Knowledge ........................................................... 204

13. THE LAST PERSON ............................................. 214
    Not All "Last" Persons Win the Race what's Gone Wrong? ................................................................. 216

# INTRODUCTION

When I gave my life to Christ and joined a local church, I noted that the term revival was the language of every Pentecostal Church. As a new Christian, I had lots of imaginations about revival since I didn't have any idea of what it meant.

Surprisingly enough, even the neighbouring nations like Kenya and others, also predicted that revival would start from their churches.

Pondering a lot about where exactly revival was to start from, I realised that it was not this enormous picture everyone was waiting for. God's desire is every church to turn back to Him and start walking in humility and obedience to His word.

Everyone has a different concept of "Revival." It became a favourite song of many churches worldwide. However, the challenge remains, who is worthy to start revival and how?

The promise of revival belongs to everyone, just as all athletes are cheered on to win a race, but, the decider is the finishing line. Many people are stuck in the waiting mode, not considering that every waiting period has an end.

Ecclesiastes 3:1
To everything there is a season, a time for every purpose under heaven.

God didn't say that revival would start from heaven and then circulate the earth. It must first start in us and then spread out through us. Jesus called the twelve and discipled them, before He sent them out as apostles to the ends of the world with the gospel of the kingdom.

In the past, we have seen many people claim to have held revival meetings, but because they themselves weren't revived, much concentration was put on building names other than God's kingdom. We cannot expect to change others if we ourselves are not changed. We can only give what we have. Once we change, then we can become role models of revival to the world.

You can read about the pastors of Budadiri East in the foothills of Sironko Valley districts in Uganda, who decided to come together as one voice called by God and commissioned by Jesus Christ, irrespective of their different ministry names.

What God is doing through them as a result of staying in God's presence is enormous. After realising that they had all heard the same call and that they couldn't get anywhere until they decided to unite their various callings into one common objective.

Looking at what I witnessed God do through them, I decided to call this book "Beautiful Beginnings from the East".

May you be blessed by God as you continued to read through this book? Amen.

# CHAPTER ONE
# WALKING ANTI-CLOCKWISE

> 1Chronicles 16:30
> Tremble before Him, all the earth. The world also is firmly established, it shall not be moved.
> Daniel 10:10
> Suddenly, a hand touched me, which made me tremble on my knees and on the palms of my hands.

Children rely on their parents for everything. When they need anything, they look to their parents. When they stumble over obstacles and get upset, they run to their parents. But when they mature and start work, they start thinking of how they can live independently. In fact some children, when they grow, develop negative attitudes towards their parents. They forget the nappy changes of their parents. Such children, when they leave home, don't look back. Irrespective of that, however negative they become, how powerful they get or how old they are, they always remain children to somebody. When people ask the number of children someone has, they don't ask of how many doctors, lawyers, prime ministers etc., but they ask the number of children. The same is true with God. He is a Father. It doesn't matter how powerful and famous someone may become, He wants that person still to rely on Him.

In most cases, when we seek God to bless us, we are willing to do whatever God requires of us spending time in prayer and reading His word. But soon as we are blessed, the blessings crowd out our appearing before God. We find ourselves too busy travelling here and there and doing other things. We have become gamblers in the kingdom instead of being heirs of the kingdom. God is not looking how busy we are for Him, but He wants us to be busy with Him. He wants us to remain His children forever.

You find many people, especially young preachers, saying, God has called them to start a revival. They think revival is about roaming around in disobedience, quoting scriptures to people rather than humbling themselves at the feet of Jesus.
God has called every single person to start a revival. However, revival can be achieved if we learn to walk anti-clockwise in the presence of God everyday so that He himself may lead us clockwise. To live anti-clockwise is to tremble at His presence while turning back to Him every second of the way.

The reason we are still waiting for revival is everyone is striving to go clockwise in our own strength without God's guidance. As everyone is engaged in striving forward to bring revival, God is also saying, "Come on, don't miss the point, revival is between me and you".

Our perception for revival has caused us to reason how to solve the puzzle, at the same time serving out of expired seasons.

It has got to the state that the more Revival has been preached, taught and prophesied, the more the church of Christ has become stubborn and complacent. While the church is being defeated in these areas, the devil is making a stand advancing against the church in every area.

Looking at the Church from a spiritual view point, is like a boa constrictor that coils itself around its prey stifling the life out of it. The devil has choked the Church from understanding the true purpose of God.

In the eighties up to mid-nineties before the revival massage became popular, people had God's fear and reverence. You could look at a reverend or pastor and see godliness in them. You could walk through a church and feel the holiness of God's presence. Today things have changed, revival has produced more thugs and robbers in the form of sheep that desire to live clockwise lives. Revival has also given people the freedom and the right to live any way they choose without being convicted of sin.

We are living in a modern world, where everything is tap and go. It is instant. Life has been simplified for almost everyone, but on top of that, the enemy has also modernised his tricks to fit in the church.

Today we are competing to live modern lives but someone born tomorrow will see this in the past. Life is so demanding. Modernity is very good, but if not lived with godly aims, it will trap many to turn away from God.

To live anti-clockwise life enables us to find God and have fellowship with him. Jesus Christ is the same yesterday today and forever. Everything in this world comes and goes but the word of God stands forever. It's like a public transport transferring people from one destination to another. In order to enjoy God's ride, we have to sit facing Jesus. Let's not be confounded with worldly things like we are here forever, but use the world to accomplish the purposes of our God who called us.

## Obstacles of Revival

Revival is God being thoughtful of His people that they may repent and turn from their wicked ways so that He may forgive them, heal the land and show himself great.

In Genesis 8:21 we see God speaking in His heart never again to curse the ground for man's sake, though the imaginations of man's heart are evil from his youth. And He said He would never again destroy every living thing as He did. When we continue reading the chapter we find that after God saying those words, He made a covenant and made the rain bow to be a sign.

It's clear that God is a God of covenant and He keeps His word. That's why we see however perverse and wicked the earth has become, God has never destroyed it. Instead, He lets the enemy increase bondages on people, with the proviso He will free them when they turn back to Him. People ask questions like, "If God is powerful, and why does He allow the devil to control His people? The devil has access to control people but when they turn back to God He sets them free.

Jeremiah 29: 10
For thus says the LORD: After seventy years are completed at Babylon, I will visit you and perform my good word toward you, and cause you to return to this place.

The place God has prepared for those who turn to Him is, His presence. Every moment we come back into the presence of God we get refreshed, restored or revived and when we stay there we become sources of revival.

## The Source

I come from the surrounding region of Lake Victoria where the source of the Nile is located in Uganda. I see many explorers and tourists come from all over the world to see the source that produces the mighty river Nile. The River Nile is a blessing to many nations and has a biblically historic background.

When you become the source of revival, you don't make posters and advertisements for people to come and be a part of it. They will just flood in every time they hear about you because you carry the presence of God.

When you become the source of revival, you will be like a rotten carcase whose smell attracts all sorts of insects, birds and animals from a distance.[Positive – honey]

The biggest challenge the church has is that it has been easy to return to the presence of God but very hard to stay in it. It's been easy to call down revival while failing to maintain it. It is simple for many to become Christians but not many have understood and obtained their Christian rights and inheritance.

I say this because I come from a background of a nation that saw and witnessed revival and the presence of God. As a nation we sought and called out to God until He came down. The fame of His presence in Uganda was heard all over the world. Our neighbouring countries were so amazed at what God was doing in Uganda. The favour of God covered our nation so specifically that some people could sense what was happening from the borders and the airport.

One time I met a Jewish man and when I told him that I was from Uganda, he said to me, are you from this small country that started a new religion spreading over the whole of Africa like fire? I was so amazed at the way the man spoke about Uganda.

Besides that, as time went by, the move of God began to subside. Christians lost the respect and the trust they carried in our nation. They began to be seen as thieves and all other ungodly-like images. The question is, where did we go wrong?

It's easier to know and remember when you are turning back to God than when you walk away from Him. That's why God wants us to walk anti-clockwise to maintain fellowship with Him while He cares for our future responsibilities.

I believe we lost the presence of God because after seeking and finding God, we stopped going back to Him and started focusing on how to acquire things.

King Saul started out with God. He had God's favour and presence before he went into battle. But when he arrived and saw a great deal of plunder, He ignored God's voice and traded it with his lustful eyes, ending up being rejected from being a King.

The bible says the voice of a king commands. Everybody does qualify to Kingship level. The downfall starts once a person forgets the purpose of God and starts focusing on acquiring material possessions. Their Kingship is traded from the voice of God with perishable things, just as Esau traded his birthright with food.

Once we turn back to God's presence, He lifts us above to become the light and the salt of our communities. During this time when we are above shining like stars, the world starts to look to us for guidance. When we fall to the worldly standard it picks faults with us and then uses them against us. Being up there is like standing in a danger zone or designated area. Either you follow the instructions to save yourself or follow your own way and get into trouble.

God told Moses to remove his shoes before He sent him to Egypt. The shoes are the preparation of the gospel of peace. God saw Moses' heart carried the burden for his people. He was the right person to send but God could not send him wearing the same shoes he left Egypt in.

Egyptian made shoes landed him and the Israelites into trouble when he tried to help them because they were not meant to bring peace. Many people have gone out to serve God, but still wearing Egyptian (worldly) made shoes. That's why instead of revival we bring shame and humiliation to the body of Christ.

Some of the troubles we landed ourselves in are that we only visited the presence of God with the burden for ministry rather than a change of lifestyle. We didn't spend time with Him to prepare us for His righteousness sake. Pharaoh is not shaken by the burdens we have, but by those who have been moulded by God's fire.

God told Moses to remove his shoes before telling him, His own plan for the people. A guest who comes to your house and removes shoes shows the interest to stay longer. But the one who stands in the door way, you know is just checking on you but has got other programs.

The world is not changing because in the past we have only gone to God to sign contracts other than seeking to be like Him. We have signed contracts and have come up with mega ministries with less spiritual impact because what we preach is not who we are.

The fact is that the world is not listening to what we preach but is eagerly watching to see us walk what we preach. This is the very world that Jesus commissioned us to reach. So how are we going to reach them in areas we are not allowed to talk about Jesus?

When the revival touched my nation, we had mega preachers with great revelations but by refusing to remove the shoes of Egypt at God's call, we have seen a lot of compromise and spiritual deaths happen.

I told God never to raise me up until He has made sure that He has dealt with my weaknesses. I prayed that I would rather serve Him in a low profile than lifting me then fall. For when we fall, it's not easy to rise or re-build the lost glory. Many people have strived to get there, before they let God deal with their weaknesses. Afterwards they have become bad news and stumbling blocks. That's why it's said that judgment will start from the house of God.

The old shoes made our fame and the glory of God fade away from my nation that now, most people preach history instead of the present presence of God.

## Competition and Strife between the Leaders

There was a time God raised up key leaders who could speak and the whole nation listened. Because there was such a hunger and thirst for the word of God, these leaders took advantage of that, to mislead people by saying things in God's name yet they were designed to fulfil their own interests. They openly competed with one another in a way that, if one of them had started a program which captured people, all others would strive to do the same.

When elephants fight it's the grass that gets destroyed. Likewise, innocent people would move around, being tossed like wind, wondering where to go since God was in every place. Paul rebuked the church and said you foolish Galatians, who bewitched you? You started in the spirit now you have ended up in the flesh.

## Greed

The spirit of mammon took over. The gospel of Christ was traded for money. People who went to pastors for counselling or prayer, were asked to bring money first. A servant of God would start preaching a good sermon, filled with revelations of the Spirit, but as he continued to minister, he started adding words about giving until the whole message became focused on money.

The Bible warns about mixing yeast and the flour. Yeast makes bread larger in size but reduces its nutritional value. The enemy knows those who are being fed with this kind of bread in times of trial so he doesn't need to do much to take them down.

Some leaders also employ the trick of making people give money quickly. They use the gimmick of explaining that God was saying there were a certain number of people with a certain amount of money to give Him. They would ask from the highest amount to the lowest, knowing that in the church there were all kinds of people, from the very rich to very poor, and would add that God wanted to bless them. Who doesn't want to be blessed? People would rush to bring in money according to their level of giving.

As though that was not enough, they would make sure that even those who didn't have anything should borrow from a friend in order to be able to give an offering. God knows if we don't have anything to give. But people were told that if they didn't give anything, they wasted their time coming to church to see others blessed by God.

You could go to churches and find a pastor getting richer and richer while the people became poor. Christians who couldn't afford to give were told to put their faith in God and not look to the pastors. What's the sense of telling someone to trust God if you already have what that person is in need of?

Some leaders also got to the point of warning people over the radio to stop coming to them if they knew they didn't have money for transport to go back to their homes. People would walk for kilometres while starving or sick but couldn't afford medicine, hoping that if only they met a pastor their needs would be solved.

## Pride

The biggest tool of pride is money. Before our leaders became wealthy they were so repentant. They were open to receive correction regardless of who

God was using to tell them. But after they accumulated wealth, most of them turned and began to do what their money could supply them even if it defied the name of God. Most servants began sinning openly that when other leaders tried to rebuke them, instead of turning back to God, they would respond through the media: "What right does anyone have to tell them what to do"?

There is nothing in this world like dealing with people who know the truth. Once you tell them what they are doing is not right, even if it is to their advantage, they quote Scriptures in an attempt to disprove your position.

It's unfortunate that some people come to God for what He has, not who He is. Some of the leaders continued to involve themselves in so many ungodly activities that it turned many people away. They no longer saw the salvation of Jesus as the way to heaven but they saw the way to stealing.

However, regardless of all the negative images, there were some men and women of God who fought to keep the seed of revival by spreading it all over the nation. Through their hard labouring and obedience to God's voice, they discovered and mentored pastors from one region of Uganda that I focused on in writing this book. These pastors found permanent residency in His presence displaying the heart of the Father.

The generation of "what God can do," preached about what God can give and led many to walk away from God because they didn't know Him. God testified to the Israelites that they saw His works but Moses, his servant, saw His face.

Moses was able to see God because he accepted removing his shoes when God asked him to and obeyed in spending time with a consuming God of fire. God is raising a generation of "who God is" worldwide because they have spent time with Him and know Him.

## Zeal

Therefore understand today that the Lord your God is a consuming fire. He will destroy them and bring them down before you; so you shall drive them down before you; so you shall drive them out and destroy them quickly, as the LORD has said to you. Deuteronomy 9:3

There were four leprous men in the kingdom of Israel. Though they had lost their feelings in their bodies, they were bold enough to go to the enemy's camp in an attempt to find survival. How they got the courage to convince themselves that their only chance of survival was in the enemy's territory is unbelievable.

During that time, while everyone, including the king, had escaped from their enemies, these leprous men composed themselves in readiness to attack their enemies.

In every circumstance that rises in life, everyone will reap positively or negatively in respect to the challenge. What I mean is that, everything we need is in the enemy's camp, but what is of importance is how we possess those needs.

In 2 Kings 7:1-15, we read, these hopeless (in the eyes of) men, sat at the entrance of the camp gate. But it was through them, victory, provision, hope, and revival was restored to the nation of Israel and her king.

The land had been stricken by famine so severe, that the king had failed to find a solution. At the same time, they were besieged by their enemies. Irrespective of their condition, these lepers agreed to use their disabilities to boldly advance into the enemy's camp. They were willing to die or live as long as they got food to survive.

Because of their bravery, God went ahead of them and caused their enemies to flee, leaving behind all their belongings, including food. God used these leprous men to save the nation because they had planned and worked together in one accord.

V6. For the Lord had caused the army of the Syrians to hear the noise of chariots and the noise of horses – the noise of a great army. So they said to one another, look the king of Israel has hired against us the kings of the Hittites and the kings of the Egyptians to attack us.

V7 therefore they arose and fled at twilight, and left the camp intact – their tents, their horses and their donkeys and they fled for their lives.

At the same time these leprous men decided to attack the camp, the king's army had given up all hope of victory. They were focusing on the severe famine that had swept the land. They didn't consider the fact that their enemies had camped somewhere, waiting for the night to fall before attacking them.

Whenever the enemy wants to destroy people's lives, he waits for them to be in a hopeless situation at a specific point, where hope and courage were fading. During this testing time, most people decide to surrender and make peace with their enemies.

There is spiritual famine in the body of Christ today, The Kingdom army has put down their weapons and are running around looking for food in an effort to survive with their families. They had forgotten that they were trained to save their nation, not just their families. The enemy had observed them from afar and had seen that they had put their weapons down. But watch and see, God is stirring up the hearts of men and women who are like the leprous men. Even though they have lost their feelings as a result of sitting in God's presence for so long, they will bring food and water back into the kingdom.

God is raising up men like David with extraordinary training and tactics to destroy the modern day Goliaths. When Goliath looked at David, he did not understand him because he didn't look like a trained soldier. He is young. He has no weapon. But David comes to him with a new weapon invented in the presence of God. No nation in the world has ever seen anything like this. God Himself trained David and gave him his invisible weapon. He had seen that the army of Israel was equipped with the same skills as their enemies and all possessed the same weapons.

This makes me pause for a while and ask myself, "Lord what is it in me that is as the same as my enemies?" I tell you, it's useless to fight an enemy who knows your source of weaknesses and strengths. The only training ground where the enemy will never understand our attack methods is in the presence of God. When we carry God's presence, we carry the whole heavenly host with us.

God has been saying for so long we have tried to use the same world system to build the church and it has failed. He is raising up a generation with His own system to bring His people back to Him. I read somewhere someone had quoted this statement that if you learn to kneel before God you will learn to stand before all men.

Isaiah 49:2-6
And He has made my mouth like a sharp sword;
In the shadow of His hand He has hidden me,
And made me a polished shaft;
In His quiver He has hidden me
And He said to me,
You are my servant, O Israel,
In whom I will be glorified '.
Then I said I have labored in vain,
I have spent my strength for nothing and in vain;
Yet surely my just reward is with the LORD,
And my work with my God.' "
And now the LORD says,
Who formed Me from the womb to be His servant,

To bring Jacob back to Him,
So that Israel is gathered to Him
(For I shall be glorious in the eyes of the LORD
And my God shall be my strength),
Indeed He says it's too small a thing that you should be my servant
To raise up the tribes of Jacob,
And to restore the preserved ones of Israel;
I will also give you as a light to the gentiles,
That you should be my salvation to the ends of the earth.

It is beyond doubt that God has promised his people great things to be done in the outpouring of His glory. In decades past we saw servants of God work themselves to the limit trying to prove to the world how powerful they were. Only they know the truth the great revival has to break out in their churches. As a result, we see continuous spirits in churches, hatred, jealousy, betrayal (conspiracy), and the list goes on. The church is so mixed up and confused that the observers don't see what it claims to be.

# CHAPTER TWO
# BEAUTIFUL BEGINNINGS

The end of a thing is better than its beginning. The patient in spirit is better than the proud.
Ecclesiastes 7:9

If you took a poll to discover the plans and dreams people have, you would be blown away by the great ideas people have. You see, most of us dream about the end of a thing and forget to dream about its beginning. The beginning rests with God. He also promises us the end results. Probably if he showed us the beginning no one would be able to respond to Him.

Funnily enough, when we pray to God concerning his plan for our lives, we don't ask him to show that plan from the beginning. We want him to show us the already made plans. That's why you see people walking around with big dreams but they don't know how to implement them.

Jeremiah 29:11.
For I know the thoughts that I think toward you, says the Lord, thoughts of peace and not of evil, to give you a future and a hope.

The challenge is in how we achieve a future and a hope according to God's Word. Many have given up and probably thought God is no longer present, or a liar since things haven't worked the way they expected. While we struggle to figure out how to achieve our dreams, God continues to confirm his word as many times as He can.

The dream of God is like a 'hide and seek' game. When He gives a promise, he wants us to go through the whole process and correct procedure to achieve, with prayer being the main key. It is our responsibility to work out the dream, to start moving forward by submitting to the Holy Spirit's direction.

You find many people still wandering in the valley of dreams and not going anywhere. They carry great names and titles that aren't as effective as they should be. The enemy goes through hid list of names and realises, people make a lot of noise because they are empty vessels.

We dig the foundation and God builds the house. If our foundations are not well laid the house collapses. Therefore, if we set beautiful beginnings, God will bring better endings.

## How do we set Beautiful Beginnings?

For who has despised the day of small things for these seven rejoice to see the plumbline in the hand of Zerubbabel. Zacharias 4:10

In most cases, the cause of people failing in ministry is not God not talking to them but division and confusion. God is not only speaking to us as an individual church or ministry. He speaks to his entire body and wants us to come together. By doing that, we would have set ourselves in the right position for God to fulfil his plan.

We should know that everything we do is not about us but God. When we continually despise one another for what they try to do, we despise the work that God wants to fulfil through us. Jesus clearly said the kingdom cannot be divided against itself and stand.

When God gave Nehemiah the burden of going back to rebuild His nation and the temple of God, Nehemiah didn't do everything alone. He gathered all the elders, the prophets, the priests and all the people. He then shared with them the plan of God for their land. The people obeyed without any of them claiming who he and his function was. They positioned themselves in their professions, trades, callings, etc., to complete the work that would look like a mountain to Nehemiah. This would lead to discouragement and probably would cause him to cease in his endeavour of finishing his task.

You cannot tell me that during that time there were no other men and women with the same burden like Nehemiah's. They all worked together for the common goal of restoring the nation of Israel and the wall of Jerusalem. They rolled away the reproach that faced the land.

Today God is asking, "Where are the men and women who are going to roll away the reproach that rests upon the church of Christ.

Africa was a very hard location for the church to break through. People were so much rooted in witchcraft, they killed even the preachers who tried to preach to them. But when the churches joined their faith and prayed together, all the satanic strongholds became powerless and many turned to God, including the witch doctors.

The Africa that was once hard ground has become a source where living waters flow. When you go to Africa, apart from the media reports of interests, you really see the presence of God and the Holy Spirit moving freely among the people.

2 Chronicles 7:14 God is saying 'If "my people" not my person. Who "are", not who is called by my name will humble "themselves", not him or her and pray and seek my face, and turn from" their" not his/her wicked ways, then I will hear from heaven, and will forgive their sin and heal their land.

The enemy has narrowed our minds into being protective of the crowds we lead even if people still live in sin. We prioritise, to not lose them, probably due to what they offer not to what God wants them to be. We no longer put our major emphasis on the Great Commission that Jesus commanded us but we aim at how we can benefit. Jesus taught a good shepherd leaves the 99 and looks for the one lost.

The great revival that the whole world is waiting for is not going to break out of a specific church. It will happen if the body of Christ will continuously seek God together as His people.

Psalm 133:1-3
Behold how good and how pleasant it is for brethren to dwell together in unity. V2 It is like the precious oil upon the head, running down on the beard, the beard of Aaron, running down on the edge of his garments. V3 It is like the dew of Hermon, descending upon the mountains of Zion, for there the Lord commands the blessing life forevermore.

We must break down those walls that have resisted and hindered the move of God to flood our streets, villages and cities. God wants to do more than what we think we have seen. He wants to bring in more than what we have got. Many are those that are blocked on the outside than those on the inside.

The beginning of a thing determines its ending. I am reminded of my school days. We would complete examinations, determining our progression to the next grade. Each of us was given a promoted or not promoted report. All those not promoted meant that the following year, they repeated the class and started learning everything over again.

There was a set percentage level that even if someone fell below this mark by just one point, he or she was deemed to have to restart everything afresh. Those who repeated the same class each year, would be nick-named according to age. The longer someone repeated the class, he or she would get familiar with the class and not progress. The purpose of repeating the class was to learn the same things that would set a beautiful beginning for the child other than taking the child to the next level and result in a bad ending.

The church of Christ is in the same situation. You can ask yourself why you go through the same thing every time or year. God wants to set a beautiful beginning for you that will determine your destiny. God is not concerned about how many times we go through challenges but His desire is that we pass the test.

We have acquired so much knowledge about God yet we cannot advance above the percentage of going to the next level. We are used to the things of God all the time because we have failed to determine our beginnings. God is not going to reveal his great and unsearchable things to us if we have continually failed to set a good starting point.

I remember how children used to pick on those who repeated the class for many years. They were given nicknames that defined them: for example, Escort – meaning they were there to see others go to the next level yet they themselves never advance there. Another name was Porridge, meaning their brains were thick like porridge restricting their ability to concentrate or think. Those names were designed to humiliate and make the failures feel worthless and inadequate.

To a church that grows dormant and complacent for not advancing into God's glory, the enemy is very ready to name it. Apparently all the humiliations the body of Christ has endured in various communities is based on our own failures. We have failed to reflect the true image of our God, the image of Oneness.

The first beautiful beginning that God set for man was to create him in His own image so that he could rule the earth and subdue the nations. Without unity, we can't reflect God's image. God did not first give man authority and bless him before He created His image in him. He first formed his image in man and then blessed him. It is the vice-versa today. People want God to bless them first and then, there after, form some sort of godliness while their hearts are far from God.

What comes in the heart first is what controls it. We cannot make God's image our beautiful beginning and expect all other things to go well with us. In most cases you find that people who put wealth and power first before God, their wealth turns into curses in disguise against their own soul and body. Wealth without God makes man his own enemy.

John 17:20-21
I do not pray for those alone, but also for those who will believe in me through their word; v21 that they all may be one, as you Father are in me, and I in you: that they also may be One in Us, that the worked many believe that you send me.

## The Voice of Jesus

I have had the opportunity to go around many churches of Christ and realised that every church has a voice of God. The Bible tells us Jesus is the Lion of Judah. The devil roars around like a lion but he is not the lion. The actual Lion with a roaring voice is Jesus.

When He ascended into heaven he left the church with that voice. The Lion cannot roar and fail to be heard scaring its enemies in the jungle.

We are examples of Christ in our cities and communities but we are not heard because the voice of Christ in us is divided. Imagine what would happen if all the voices in the body of Christ roar as one voice under the government of the Prince of Peace.

We have seen Moslems capture our governments' attention and cause the main streets in cities, to be blocked during their prayer time due to the sounding of one voice. We don't see them with small groups, each with its vision contradicting one another. They all follow the vision of Islam and they work together to see it fulfilled. The vision of Prophet Muhammad is to make every human being Islamic and worship Allah.

We have suppressed the vision of our Lord Jesus to every man having his own ideologies to achieve the earthly pleasures.

The pastors of Budadiri East, after realising how much time and years they had wasted trying to build their own ministries, how hard they had laboured with less impact in the communities, decided to go back to the foundation of unity and then begin afresh.

They managed to tackle every challenge or hardship that faced any ministry as one body in Christ. They have achieved great results in a short period of time, which would have taken one ministry many years to achieve.

They also birthed the agape love of Christ among Christians. Christians support one another and fellowship together as the body of Christ. Many people have given their lives to Christ every day and churches are rapidly increasing.

Pastors are no longer dreaming of small things they could achieve in their churches, but all have one mind of a great dream they want executed in the community. They have broken the mindset of the four corner barriers of their churches.

The presence of God is so evident among them with signs and wonders, miracles and healings. It is no longer history to them but is a very real and present fact.

When God's overflow comes down, the church will not have enough room to sustain it, but it will flow and fill all the empty vessels in the city.

Daniel 11:32
Those who do wickedly against the covenant, he shall corrupt with flattery: but the people who know their God shall be strong, and carry out great exploits.

I prayed to God as to how I could share this experience of His move in this unknown community and I felt led to combine everything in this book. My prayer to God is while you read this book, he may open your eyes to see, your mind to understand and your heart to shift into yearning to see the full blessings of God come upon the body of Christ, so that the world may witness his latter glory. Amen.

# CHAPTER THREE
# BUDADIRI EAST PASTORS

Jeremiah 23:2
Therefore thus says the Lord God of Israel against the shepherds who feed my people: you have scattered my flock, driven them away, and not attended to them. Behold, I will attend to you for the evil of your doings, says the Lord.

I was born and raised up in Budadiri East, a constituency that is composed of five counties, forty sub-counties and the population of 100,000 people. Growing up as a young girl, I saw the status of the church was held in very low esteem, Christians were called lunatics and composed of people who wasted their time. Churches weren't giving any good example to the community, even though they held crusades and evangelized door to door about the love of Jesus who died for our sins. James says 'faith without works is dead'. If one person in the whole community was converted, it would be misunderstood as to the person having made a very big mistake.

One day while I was at high school, one of my friends gave his life to Christ and joined one of the churches. My friends and I felt pity for him and we did everything to get him out of the church.

This wasn't a good move because after that he left school, became an alcoholic, and a few years later he died of AIDS.

It was until I gave my life to Christ that I realised how woeful I was, inflicting my friend, causing him to go to hell. I felt terrible then, but today when I share the good news about God's love to sinners, I don't get ashamed. I vowed to God that it was through me that his precious soul went astray and so I want him to use me to win many to his kingdom.

Pastors had led a very bad example in the community that there was no way whatsoever any one would desire to become a pastor or a servant of God. They could verbally fight and say nasty words to each other and could use the word of God to preach against others.

They told the congregations not to go to other churches that were not of their doctrine for they would be considered as unbelievers who needed to repent again and accept Christ. This was so serious that if one church had a meeting or a crusade on the other side of the land, the other church would also organise the same not far from the location where they were and even conduct their meetings on the same dates.

They would also advertise the same message on posters but different churches. Specifically, there were two that were separated by a wall. One time I walked by and heard them singing the same song at the same time. The sound was so ugly that I couldn't hear any word other than confusion and overwhelming noise. I asked myself why they didn't unite, since they were praising the same God and reading the same Bible. This was occurring in order to stop Christians going to other meetings.

Once we deviate from God's purpose, we start to struggle to do things our way. There were times, if one church converted new believers to their church, other churches would follow up the new converts and try to win them to their churches by telling them negative things about the church that witnessed to them.

Some of the new believers would prefer not to go to any church or stay with the first one and tell the pastor what other church tried to do.

I remember after I had given my life to Christ, (thank goodness none of the pastors led me to Christ as I was one of those who didn't like them.)I went to one of the churches on a Sunday. I was so shocked that instead of seeing them being happy that God had brought these people from Kampala to preach, and through them many people had come to the Lord and filled their church. Instead, they went and invited their then, "overseer" (bishop) to come and rubbish the group from Kampala just because they were not part of their organisation.

The bishop began to criticize them for bringing the young boys and girls, who he believed were prostitutes and thieves who go around looking for men and money. He rubbished the preachers for not being mature in God's things therefore they didn't deserve to preach.

I said to myself but these are the very people who lead me here. What then am I doing here if that's the case? I thought that I was the only one disgusted and I decided to walk out of the service to go home.

To my surprise all the people who had gone there also decided to walk out. It was like as if everyone was waiting for me to get out before they followed. Everyone was so disappointed in the bishop that some people decided over their dead bodies to never go to any church.

I thank God that even though that had happened I didn't give up my Christ. I was consumed with His Love and I wanted to know more about him. God had chosen me and loved me. He began sending his servants from different parts of Uganda and Kenya to come and mentor me with the word of God in the church I was happy in.

Before I formed you in the womb, I knew you: Before you were born I sanctified you, ordained you a prophet to the nations.

## Why did we choose This Church?

There were a big number of us who had given our lives to Christ through the crusade. Every church we went to, the pastors were telling us nothing productive other than trying to warn us not to go to other churches because they were living in disobedience, (they broke away from other churches). The other church was not good enough so they decided to go and start their own. They didn't teach a good word from the Bible, they didn't pray and cast out demons, or perform any wonderful acts.

Of all the pastors who came to us, there was a particular pastor, his church was the most despised, disvalued and disregarded among other churches. This pastor had never gone to school and didn't speak any English, so he was considered as not knowing anything.

When he came to us he wasn't talking against any church or pastor. He wasn't showing us any hatred or competition, but he was actually so loving and caring. He used to teach us the word of God. His word was one of hope. It was so powerful and full of promise, we felt empowered to start serving God.

Now remember, his church was only small and full of old and very poor people. He didn't have money and he was struggling to build the church. So one Sunday we decided to go to his church and guess what? Even if his church was grass thatched, even when it rained we swam in mud, we felt a belonging to that place. God had taken us there to go and be blessed to become a blessing.

We then decided to team up with our pastor to do the things that needed to be done. The next week we collected the poles and the roofing to build the church. We built it within one week and then began to collect money to buy seats and drums for our church.

God used us under the supervision and guidance of our pastor that many more people started coming to church. We started going out to preach the gospel of Jesus with power and many people came to the Lord and saw miracles and healings everywhere we went.

Basically pastors are meant to disciple and nurture the calls that God puts in his people to function effectively.

If pastors are not following the true principles of God on how to raise ministers, they will raise ministers with hatred, division, greed, and without God's fear, full of pride and self- seeking.

We gave what we had. If you want to know the heart of any pastor, you will see it in the believers he leads. If the pastor has love, you will see rivers of love flowing out of people. If the pastor is a giver, the people will always give generously. There is no way a man is going to hide what is in him even if he tries to pretend. There is a saying that if a venomous snake hides in a hole and you want it out, pour hot chilli in the hole. The chilli makes it rush out regardless of the troubles ahead. A man's character cannot hide his identity.

Jesus said we will know His own by their fruit. I guess he knew that many would try to hide in Him but a fruit cannot disguise itself into a different fruit. A mango brings forth a mango.

I believe God saw that he had chosen us for the great work and if he left us under the leadership of those pastors, we would have not grown up to become who we are. He chose this humble pastor who was a no-body before the eyes of men, to pass on to us a godly character in Him that we may become who we are today.

## Hatred

Wherever hatred dominates, grace and love are replaced with criticism and judgement. Jesus did not come to judge anyone but he came that all may be saved. How many children of God, when we see people we have issues with, go through hard times, we don't pray for them but we say God is judging them.

There was a time when one of the pastors lost a child every year for four years. I believe if pastors had come together and asked God why this was happening, God would have revealed to them the cause and brought healing to this devastated family.

Who knows, maybe this man of God was going through a trial time. We all know very well that even the righteous are tried by the devil. Many are the troubles of a righteous man but the Lord delivers him from all. The story of Job is the perfect example to make us understand why God's people have to suffer sometimes.

Job 2:3
Then the Lord said to Satan, have you considered my servant Job, that there is no one like him on the earth, a blameless and upright man, one who fears God and shuns evil? And still he holds fast to his integrity, although you incited me against him to destroy him without cause.

V4 So Satan answered the Lord and said, skin for skin. Yes, all that a man has he will give for his life.

V5 But stretch out your hand now, and touch his bone and his flesh, and he will surely curse you to your face!

V6 and the Lord said to Satan, "behold he is in your hand, but spare his life."

V7 So Satan went out from the presence of the Lord and struck Job with painful boils from the sole of his foot to the crown of his head.

The Bible tells us to carry one another's burdens. But in this pastor's case every one came up with his/her own allegations. Others sat in God's judgment seat and judged him for not obeying God.

Others said he had sacrificed his children to the devil for riches. They said he had gone under the sea and encountered the devil who asked him for his children.

Initially, there was a belief in Africa that people who get rich or seek to get rich go under the sea to make vows with Lucifer to make them rich. And one of the signs of fulfilling the vows was someone losing children, a partner, or close family members.

This was a very hard and trying moment for the pastor as he didn't have anybody to stand by him.

Non-believers don't create their own words to attack the church of Christ. They actually quote from what has been told by Christians who speak against each other.

When you are a Christian remember that not all your family members or friends are saved.

The non-believers got those words spoken by other Christians and used them as a platform to ridicule and attack the entire body of Christ.

Believers should note that anything they do or speak against each other or other churches actually kills themselves and conspires against their own bodies.

The Bible says we are all members of the body of Christ. Just as much as you love yourself you can endure your own mistakes without criticising or denying yourself. So is being patient with each other. Love, supporting and respecting them, irrespective of their wickedness or hatred will never solve any problem.

Romans 12:5
So we being many are one body in Christ, and individually members of one another.

1 Corinthians 12:12
For as the body is one and has many members but all the members of that one body, being many, are one body, so also is Christ.

V13
For by one Spirit we were all baptized into one body – whether Jews or Greeks, whether slaves or free – and have all been made to drink into one Spirit.

Ephesians2:14-16
For he himself is our peace, who has made both one and has broken down the middle wall of separation, v15 having abolished in his flesh the enmity, that is the law of commandments contained in ordinances so as to create in Himself one new man from the two, thus making peace, v16 and that He might reconcile them both to God in one body through the Cross, thereby putting to death the enmity.

## Division

A seed is sown in the ground and germinates. It grows into a big tree with many branches, but that doesn't stop it from bearing the same fruit. Jesus is the seed of all our faith. Therefore, there has to be a cord or anchor that binds us together from falling apart.

I have listened to many preachers say that division is good, giving the example of Paul and Barnabas when they parted, everyone continued with the work of God.

If you read this chapter carefully, you realise that they both had godly intentions. It was not a result of them having misunderstandings over money, power and all the other lame excuses people use today to promote disunity in the body of Christ.

Understand how genuine diversity works. Jesus commissioned us to go and multiply to make disciples of all nations. I know that when a church grows it produces the five-fold ministry and then sends these ministries out to multiply and do more work. Here you can see the blessing and the principle of God flowing.

However there are churches which have started as a result of sin. A pastor tried to rebuke or chasten someone over something he did. He decided to break away with a number of Christians and go and start his own thing. This is the biggest disease which has degraded the value of a church in communities.

These days everyone has freedom of speech, expression and worship in our world but with God His word and principles remain the same. What will a man gain in gaining the whole world and losing his soul?

Jesus said many will come to me saying Lord, Lord I did this, but He will say to them go away from my presence, I didn't know you. As much as the world has given us a lot of freedom, we must remain conscious of the word of God.

Division has misdirected us from the purpose of God for our lives. I have one of my sons that I brought up in church. As a youth he did something that through it, he was influenced by other people to go to other churches where he was not known. But he decided to stay in church and step down from ministering. He was under discipline and accepted everything he was told to do.

Today you tell a Christian who is anointed by God to sit under discipline for some reason, you are looking for war. That's why pastors no longer waste their time warning people, because if they did they can be harassed. They can even be sued to court. I sometimes wonder why we allow people we don't want to obey lead us.

As my son gave up everything to seek God's forgiveness God raised him up again and blessed him with a school.

Basically, as a ministry God had promised to give us a school but we didn't know how this was going to be fulfilled as I am not a teacher and I didn't have a heart to run a school. God gave me the plan of a school but He didn't ask me to start one.

Therefore, He had my son, who decided to run away or felt like he should go and start his own church, under influence. Would we have achieved the promise of God of a school? We would both be running a divided mission, but his obedience in God's chastening has produced great results. That even when God took me out of church for other responsibilities, he was the one standing as a pillar others could rely on for the direction of the ministry because he was there from the beginning.

When you go in disobedience, be well assured that one day the same will be done to you, for you reap what you sow.

Job 3:8
Even as I have seen those who plot iniquity and sow trouble reap the same.

I am not against having many churches, but we see so many mushrooming churches almost in every corner of the nation, yet the real blessing of God is not seen.

What concerns me is, in these days, we see many churches starting but no people coming to Christ. Can't we really stop and ask ourselves what are we doing? The people filling new churches are transfers from other churches. They are not willing to be committed and be accountable for their mistakes. In Uganda we call them, prostitute Christians. They go from church to church picking faults with pastors, other Christians and criticise everything they find in the church. In the main, such people have issues with themselves in that they don't want to be accountable, but they themselves would rather bring others to account.

When churches are not functioning together in unity, these people begin stirring trouble and wars between them by "splitting hairs" on words.

Division causes people to be vagabonds. They don't stay in one place but wander all around and never develop in the Spirit because they have never been exposed to sound teachings. Such people become dangerous in that the fragments of Word they get from different churches are put together and formed into half-baked doctrine.

When pastors work together in unity, they understand Christians from all other churches. Pastor, God did not call you to pastor and care for only your four walls of your churches, you are called to look after the whole flock of Jesus.

Jesus asked Peter three times if he loved Him. He required him to care of His flock, not to just care for his ministry or organisation. When we start caring for God's flock irrespective of which church we belong, God will take care of our ministries.

One time we went to a particular church to fellowship there. We introduced ourselves and explained that we were Christians and so we thought we had joined them, becoming one with them.

After a few weeks we were given a consent form requiring us to submit to their doctrine. At first when I tried to integrate with other Christians, I noticed people were looking at us with curious eyes. Looking through the form, the woman who was meant to assist me understand said to me, before you become our member, you must do our DNA course to qualify you to understand our doctrine.

I wondered why their DNA was different from the word of God.

You see, man will always try to create something to make it difficult between others and God. God did not send us to go and introduce courses that make it hard for others to worship or serve him.

Such man-made ideologies have also contributed to the division of the body of Christ. We all belong to and serve Christ but we all don't have the same beliefs. Why, and how many Christs do we serve? Don't we see that we are going to be shocked when He appears instead of rejoicing at His return?

The world wonders if truly God exists. A body not divided against itself stands. However, all parts of the body may have different functions but at the end of the day they all need each other. The hand cannot do what the foot can, nor the eye what the mouth can, but each part of the body is just as useful as every other part of the body.

These parts are created to fulfil each other's need. If the mouth wants to eat, it's the hand that feeds and if the hand wants to wash the face, it's the foot that walks to where the water is. Let the common things we see teach us the things of God.

Don't think that because you have got your own doctrine you have got everything. You will be surprised to find out that you need other people's ministries in your church in order to function effectively. Christ is coming to take one Church, not many churches under his umbrella.

When God called me, He told me that there were so many churches which have been opened, yet My people have not yet changed. There is still a lot of work to be done inside the church as well as outside the church. He said, if the inside people will change then it will be easy for the outside to change. He said, I therefore send you forth that whenever you go to various places, don't start new churches but stand with my people whom I have placed there to do my work. You should only open churches in unreached places where the people don't have anywhere to go.

In this massage we see that the heart of Jesus is focusing on the unchanged souls bogged in churches. And here we are rushing to open churches everywhere because we want to be recognised as ones with many churches. What does it profit by having a church that is full of unchanged people who moved away from other churches, because they stubbornly refused to change?

We are deceiving ourselves with the numbers, yet the value is less. It's like having sacks of money that has no value and will never make you rich, we toil in vain. The Bible says on that day when Jesus returns everyone will appear before God, giving account.

I come from a coffee growing area but before the coffee arrives in the factory, it goes from the farmer, then to the local small business owners and then, finally to the factory. So it's the small business owners' responsibility to make sure they get good coffee from the farmers so that they don't make losses besides all the expenses they incur in transport to the factory. When it arrives, the coffee is sorted, the good from the bad. The factory then buys the good quality coffee and lets the farmers take back the bad coffee, or throws it away.

Every pastor or church leader will be shocked on that day when you stand before God to present your harvest. After all the time you have invested in people who just fill the church and don't want to change, you will watch them being sorted and thrown into hell as you realise you are left with nothing and without reward.

There are some places where I go and God uses me mightily in churches. Afterwards people demand me to open a church for them. I asked them the reason why they wanted a new church and they said because they didn't want to lose the fire I had brought to them. But I told them to stay in their churches and keep the fire burning.

I simply know that God didn't ask me to start churches and I don't serve God based on people's demands. I told them that God does not take me to churches to cause division but to build on what was started and to add that which was lacking.

To me starting new churches feels like rewinding the move of God and disorganising His plan. Some churches don't start as a result of God asking them but when someone goes somewhere then God uses him/her for a specific purpose, they end up sliding from grace and think they are much better. They look at themselves as the saviours of the hour, that if they don't do something people are going to perish in churches. Such churches are of the type that have risen like wildfire in the forest and within a short period they go as cold as ice. When you search for their remains you can't find them.

When people see the grace of God in you, they will try to lure you into doing many things that God had not asked you to do. Many servants of God are lying dormant, struggling to do things that God never asked them to do. If you see yourself struggling to do things, give yourself a break, and ask God to give you clear direction. I have learned not to struggle or strive for the things of God. Because if God says he will do something, He surely does so without me sweating or stressing myself about it.

Psalm 37:7
Rest in the Lord, and wait patiently for Him; do not fret because of him who prospers in his way. Because of the man who brings wicked schemes to pass.

Matthew 11:29-30
Take my yoke upon you and learn from me, for I am gentle and lowly in heart, and you will find rest for your souls.

V30 For my yoke is easy and my burden is light.

## Greed

Luke 11:39
Then the Lord said to him, "Now you Pharisees make the outside of the cup and dish clean, but your inward part is full of greed and wickedness.

One time the Lord gave me the chance to see how greed consumes the church of Christ. t was in 2009, while fasting and praying for forty days without food but only liquids. It was on the 39th day of my fast, the Lord gave me a dream. In this dream, I saw we were many people gathered in a wide city square.

In the city square there was a king sitting on his throne. On the right of his throne was a big crowd of Christians and on the left were Muslims. He was sitting watching what the two sides were doing.

It came to giving time and two big baskets were brought forward on each side. I saw that on the Muslim side they were excitedly rushing to fill their basket, everyone including the poor were pushing through to put something in the basket. Within short time the basket was overflowing and those who couldn't manage to come closer to the basket were throwing money from the back.

But when I looked at the Christian basket, very few people were just dragging themselves slowly to put very little money, mostly coins. On the Christian side, I saw some people walking around with their small baskets collecting money from people. They were convincing them that they too, need money for their own ministries.

While that was still going on, I looked at the Muslims. They were very happy celebrating, hugging one another speaking loud. "We will continue to collect more money as much as we can to support our leader Osama bin Laden" to take over the world.

Some of you may say that Osama bin Laden is dead. I want to tell you that his name represents the spirit of radical Muslims that are terrorising people. He is the one who started that move so even if he is dead his vision still continues.

I saw that on the left side of the Muslims was a great sea. A big wave came and cast half of them into the sea. The remnants encouraged themselves saying, "Even though some of us have been killed, we are not going to give up until we turn the whole world into Islam".

I looked back to the king, who I believe was Jesus Christ, He was in tears and so devastated that he couldn't look at Muslims overpowering Christians. He got up sobbing and addressed the Christians. He said "I placed you on the safe side. I favoured you above everyone, but you couldn't do anything. You have got everything to overpower these people but because you are divided and so greedy, they are stealing what belongs to you.

As he said this, the Muslims cheered and continued to shout as they advanced towards the Christians. They began to prosper by having good schools and better projects that attracted the children of Christians to them.

While the Christian children were in the Muslim gatherings, I saw the Christian fathers coming in with big sticks and they began to whip their own children in anger for going there. The more they tried to beat their children, the more things grew from bad to worse. They lost everything to the Moslems who cared for and cherished them.

The dream finished while the Christians were so distressed because they had lost everything to the Muslims.

This dream is self–interpreting. The Bible says let those who have ears, hear what the Spirit of God says to the Church. All the things that happened in the dream are already happening. We see Muslim bombings in public gatherings. They are buying churches to turn them into powerful mosques and other projects in the west.

When you see an abomination standing in the holy place, know that the Son of man is about to come. Islam is rapidly taking over western nations that used to send missionaries to the whole world with the good news of Jesus Christ.

I was so terrified by the dream that I began to cry. My husband asked me why I was crying but it was too overwhelming for me to explain. I kept saying, the dream. "Christians if we don't learn to sacrifice now and save our position, the time is coming when we will lose everything unless someone chooses to become a Muslim. I say this from a background of a nation that was once under the leadership of a Moslem president, Idi Amin Dada. During his regime he wanted all Ugandans to become Moslems and those who didn't want were assassinated. Very many Christians lost their lives and others left the country.

The spirit of greed functions in the way that people want to receive so much but they don't want to give. You can't harvest from where you did not sow. Christians are so alert to the receiving side, yet, at the same time, we don't want to sacrifice.

When you invite a preacher to come and minister in any meeting, you have to bargain how much you will pay him first. Didn't Jesus say, if you look after my business, I will look after you? Didn't he promise his disciples not to carry anything, because he was going to provide for them?

These days we do the work of God for reward with conditions, not as a call. If you hold a call of God in you, it's like a baby who wants to be born. The baby doesn't give the mother conditions of where it wants to be born but it just happens anywhere, anytime.

If truly God Himself called us to serve Him, why do we put burdens on others? I think we should be looking for opportunities to fulfil the call of our Master. We should be walking around like a desperate hen looking for a spot to lay an egg. We are no longer concerned about the hungry souls but we are worried about our hungry stomachs.

Many times I have been invited to the meetings where the pastor dictates to me to talk about money and not the revelation of the Holy Spirit. I ask them to tell me why they want to focus on the money gospel? The answer I get is that would to be able to facilitate the ministry, but in actual fact they seek to use it for their own pleasures.

In Uganda, they had this saying that a shepherd eats of his flock. This may be true but they shouldn't eat parts of a sheep while it's still alive.

No wonder people are so sick of hearing about money all the time. The most boring time is when we talk about money every Sunday to the same people. People have heard the gospel of giving until it's falling out of their noses. Focusing too much on anything is always dangerous. Even manna from heaven became too much for the Israelites who were living by faith.

One time I organised a crusade and used my money to invite a dynamic man of God to come and preach. The people were so eager waiting to hear from Him, some of them were saying when he comes they were going to give their lives to the Lord.

I went to him with a yearning heart to see people get saved and I so desperately wanted him to come. The first question he asked me was how much money was I going to pay him? Was I willing to fuel his car and incur all the costs in case his car breaks down? What kind of food was I going to feed him and what type of accommodation was I going to provide for him? He put himself ahead of God's purpose that he was called to minister to.

I am not saying that Christians don't deserve good things. The point is, even if God had raised him up he should have been flexible in all conditions for the sake of the gospel. These questions so disturbed me that I felt embarrassed before him and walked away in tears.

I guess he asked me those questions while weighing up my response. He despised me in that I couldn't afford to host him because he was a renowned man of God. Who was I? A nobody from nowhere who would dare attempt to invite him? But praise be to our God that He does not let his people down. God sent another man of His who was willing to serve regardless. He did a great work that in a week, over three hundred people gave their lives to Christ. Miracles and healing happened and God blessed his people.

God will never send a person who sets his own standards before Him. He replaces then with someone else who is willing to do His work.

Elijah thought that he was the only prophet left in the land, but to his surprise, God told him that He had 7000 more prophets hiding in the land.

While serving God we have to know that the best servants are yet to come. Whether you are a great Tele-Evangelist preacher with a mega Church, we all serve God with trembling and fear knowing that there are those still hidden in the Lord. God is still hiding some of His people, waiting for time when so-called ministries start setting themselves boundaries and He then reveals them. Don't think to yourself that no one can get where you are.

When King Saul begun to disobey God he thought he was the only king who was sought for by the Prophet Samuel. He didn't think that the same Samuel who sought to anoint him would also seek to anoint David who was busy in the fields tending his Father's flock.

Some people look at themselves and consider where they have walked and think that no one else can walk that same journey

I want to tell you that you may be the one whom Samuel anointed while you were looking for the lost asses but there are those ones He is going to anoint because they are looking after their Father's flock.

There is a difference between looking for lost asses and looking after the Father's flock. Looking "for" means, running after the amusements or pleasures of this world thinking they will add joy and happiness to you, forgetting that all those things are just temporary.

But looking "after" is obeying in God's presence taking the responsibility of His will.

The asses represent the pleasures of this world. They rate first, therefore, they also show people who are looking to gain material possessions quickly without working for them. Asses are here symbolical of horses. Betting on horses in developed nations is a very significant pastime.

In some nations, a national horse racing day brings the whole nation to standstill. People bet on different horses. When a horse wins, the bettor wins money on it.

Saul was looking for the worldly gains. Can you imagine, God sending for Saul who was looking for the lost asses, to come and lead the lost Israelites, who demanded to be ruled by a King instead of a prophet. The king represents the flesh and the pride of men but the Prophet represents the voice of God.

Sometimes you have to discern when people come asking you to do some things for them. God has allowed many churches to function under His anointing, but care should be taken where some may be Saul's leading the lost Israelites other than David tending the Father's flock.

When a man gets to the level where he feels he has acquired wisdom and everything this world affords, he no longer wants to hear from God but he wants to do everything to please his flesh. Therefore, because people wanted a king, God gave them Saul who would not listen to the voice of God but did everything to please himself.

When God told him to destroy the enemy and their belongings, he looked at taking advantage of God's victory to gain wealth. His goal for the battle was different from God's. Because of his disobedience, in the end he suffered the consequences.

It is great for God to call us but the state or position He finds us in is what matters. He can find you in the middle of rebellion or fornication and He calls you as a sign to lead rebels or fornicators. I want to tell you that whatever the case maybe at the end we are going to be accountable to God. God is not impressed by how many people we lead in our churches but by how many souls we lead to righteousness.

I have known that we cannot lead others in what we are not. Many preachers don't want to be told anything because they affirm they know what they are called to do. Saul didn't listen to Samuel even though he was called and anointed by God.

Matthew 6:24-25 No one can serve two masters. For either he will hate the one and love the other, or else he will be loyal to the one and despise the other. You cannot serve God and mammon.

After Saul's downfall God sent for David to be anointed. He was busy in the fields fighting lions and bears that tried to attack his Father's flock while his big brothers were at home. He could have used the animals and the loneliness of the field as an excuse to disobey his father.

God searches the hearts. He saw humility and a caring heart in David and decided to send Samuel to anoint him. God saw that he would be the right person to lead His people according to His voice because he had been obedient to his biological father irrespective of the risks.

When God called David, He called him as a prophet to stand in the role of a King. The reason I call him a prophet is because even when he attacked Goliath, he quoted the Word, his strength was in the name of God. He managed to win all his battles because he relied on the Word of the prophets. He inquired from God before he could do anything even if it looked like there was no need to inquire from God.

God will never get tired of us enquiring from Him as long as we do the right thing by Him and it keeps us in His presence.

## Pride

1 Peter 5:5
Likewise you younger people, submit yourselves to your elders. Yes all of you be submissive to one another and be clothed with humility, for God resists the proud, but gives grace to the humble.

We are now living in a world where everything is easily accessible. It's just a click and press of a button and everything is delivered at the door. Having all these things has made us to no longer need anybody. We no longer seek God like we ought too. We no longer listen to those that God has put over us. We only want them to speak words that are in our favour.

Pride says, you know and have more than him, therefore he has to listen or do as you please otherwise you will not tithe or give to any church program.

Pride is a very cunning spirit that takes us unaware. Jesus warned and said if we knew when the thief will come we would have closed our doors and maybe stayed at home. When the enemy wants to destroy someone, he sneaks in through the mind and all of a sudden you see him the spirit of pride manifesting through the victim's behaviour.

It's hard for the people who are dominated by pride to realise their mistakes when they are falling but instead they get easily offended.

Jesus said we should be His example because His spirit is gentle and humble .Jesus, having known the mission he had come for, had all the power and the authority to resist those who persecuted him to death. But he remained humble before God. He didn't justify himself by asking God to send his power to destroy them. He remained humble, even on the cross amidst much pain and agony, he asked God to forgive His persecutors.

Pride has caused many servants of God to manipulate people by controlling them because they are anointed ones of the Lord even when they live in sin. Pride of our hearts has also caused many to walk away wounded and broken into pieces yet at the same time we are so proud of our serving God.

When God called me into ministry, there were some things I asked him never to let me in. One of them was pride, as I could see many ministers rise in power and then, in a very short time, they fall. I didn't want to be like them for I had sacrificed a lot, including my education to follow after God.

So after praying one night I went to sleep and I had a dream that someone was showing me a very ugly animal which looked like a pig covered with mud but its face was different. He said, "Never ever let that animal get inside you". I asked him, "How could that big animal get inside me for I am only small?" He said, "That's a spirit of pride. When it enters you it destroys everything good in you, just like a pig." He said, "It's a very ugly spirit to behold and once it finds its way in, it makes you look big and ugly before people however small you maybe. That's why most people who have it, were unaware of its presence until it enters them often when they are in a time of a great deal of trouble and distress."

Many people have failed to attain the fullness of God's plan for their lives because of pride. They start well but when pride takes over they begin to think that they know everything so they don't need any guidance or counselling.

Pride is out there to sabotage the plans of God. The devil is ready to steal, kill and destroy. Once our hearts are controlled by pride, we no longer do things according to the leadership of the Holy Spirit. Our flesh contradicts the Spirit. Pride is accelerated by the things of the flesh. If we consider the majority of people, you will find that their main goal is not to reflect the image of God but they serve to gain popularity. They work hard to see that their ministries become the best or the biggest in the community, in order that many see how powerful they are. It's not a bad thing to have a big church but our motives for having a big church is the issue that is at stake here.

God's will is for us to multiply and be fruitful, but He doesn't want us to usurp His glory. You hear people say that their church is the best or the biggest in the city. We can claim the best and the biggest positions, but when mosques and other ungodly clubs increase beyond their endeavours, that means nothing to God.

It appears to bring glory to our God if the body of Christ becomes the biggest and the light of our cities. Overpowering all other beliefs. It saddens me to see people claiming positions when other religions and evil are overtaking them.

The light shone in darkness and darkness couldn't comprehend it. We are supposed to be the light of God in a dark world that people can see and run to. But you see thousands of people walking away from churches because they cannot see the light.

Many in the world don't know God, others believe He does not exist. Didn't Jesus say that the world will know Him through us, His people? Why are those people not coming to us who have the light and who are the salt of the world? A true Christian shows the flavour of salt and light by attracting many to Jesus Christ.

Light attracts many insects from the dark and when they enter they don't go back. Some die from at that point. How many people have you attracted to Christ even before the pastor notices their presence in church? You are already their role model. Once you lead someone to Christ, you become their best teacher and role model.

Many times we excuse ourselves saying that people don't want to come to Christ because they don't like Him. The Bible clearly tells us that everywhere Jesus went, thousands responded to

Him. Now, if the same Christ lives in us, what then is hindering people from coming to Him? I believe people love Christ but they don't like the way we conduct ourselves.

Hebrews 13:8
Jesus Christ is the same yesterday, today and forever.

Pride says others have failed and you are the only one to have succeeded. It is time we break the barriers of pride and seek the move of God. Never call yourself the best when the whole body of Christ is suffering defeat.

Esther is the best example who would have used her position. She is the woman who passed all the beauty tests with flying colours. Even when she was highly favoured by the king, she still kept a low profile and remained connected to her people. She remained obedient to her poor uncle, whose daily survival was to sit at the entrance of the gate (the beautiful gate) to watch the true citizens and the royals entering the city. She could have said, "Now I am a queen and everyone must listen to what I say."

It is true that when God exalts us, He puts us in positions where others listen, but that doesn't mean we stop listening to them, because it is through them the revival of a nation might appear.

A true man of God must listen to his people and the advice they have to give. Sometimes God works this way because in your position you may be too busy with other things to notice what the enemy may be planning to do. I have seen some churches whose pastors fall apart because when God used a Christian to warn them against something, they respond saying, why didn't God speak to me Himself? Pride says you are a man of God why should you listen to a lowly Christian whom you lead.

As Esther listened to her uncle, God used her to bring victory and promotion to her people. Let not pride drive you away from the purpose of God for your life and those that you are called to lead.

I heard this true story. There was a girl who suffered terribly in her life. Through her sufferings, everyone including her best friends, walked away from her except her mother and her family. She made a lot of mistakes but still they stood by her side, just as blood is thinker than water.

Now it came to pass that she got married to a very rich man and after that, instead of helping those people who stood with her during those darkest times, she started criticising her family before her husband. She made sure her husband would not give anything to anyone in her family including her mother.

We can hide things but we cannot hide our character. After some time, the man began to see some bad habits in her and decided to leave her with nothing. Now because she had elevated herself and wouldn't listen to any one, she was left alone. The pride of her heart had turned the whole circle to her troubles. It also made her to lose all the good plans God had for her.

Proverbs 16-18

Pride goes before destruction and a haughty spirit before a fall.

God can bless us but if we don't know what to do with those blessings, they can become curses in our lives. Every blessing God gives us contains His purpose. Had this girl remembered the good things others did for her, even if this man had left her, she would still have had people around her. Who knows, maybe God brought this man into her life for the sake of the entire community.

It's very important to ask God to reveal the purpose of the blessings he gives us before we think of ourselves. Blessings are not meant to drive us away from God but they are purposed to bring us closer to Him.

Jacob managed to steal Esau's blessing because Esau had walked away from his father's house and wasn't concerned about the generational family blessing, he was thinking about himself. He didn't even stop and think about his future generation. All he was worried about was now. "I want it now".

But Jacob, who knew the secret of generational blessings, kept fighting for the birthright by keeping himself close to the family until he obtained it. Jacob was willing to forsake everything and cut himself off from outdoor activities to stay near his mother and listen to what she had to say to him.

We saw in the dream when Jesus said that the Muslims were out to steal our rights, those rights were not originally meant for Jacob, but because

Esau was always pursuing the things that satisfy his flesh, he lost it.

Pride can make you thirst and hunger for worldly things. How will people know that you are a man of God without driving the most expensive car? As I said before, it's good for us to have expensive things, but we need to acquire them genuinely. If you are a woman or man of God you don't have to rely on the things you can see. A true man or woman of God cannot hide. It's better to be discerned as a servant of God than being seen by people.. We miss God's visitation in the way we look at things.

One time there were two men of God, who desperately went to seek God in the closet. They fasted and called on Jesus to visit them so that they might know He had called them. Finally the Holy Spirit visited them and promised to visit them in their homes. So they went home to wait for Jesus' visitation.

A very old filthy man came and knocked at one of the men's door. When he opened it he saw the old man and asked him what he wanted. The man asked him for drinking water. He said, "I am afraid I don't have a cup I can put water in for you. All my nice cups are for my special guests. Even now I am expecting one whom I don't want to find you here."

The man said, "I have been walking for a very long time, can't you give me a place in the shade to rest for a while?" He said, "Go and try somewhere else, as I told you I have a guest I am expecting soon." The old man walked away and went to the other man's place. When he knocked on the door, the man opened and quickly invited him in with joy. When he entered and wanted to sit on the floor. He was told, "No, no, these seats are for all my guests. You are my special guest, can I serve you a drink?" He rushed and got him a glass of water and then served him with some of the food he had cooked for his guest. After the old man had finished eating, he prayed a blessing on the family and then left.

As he was walking out the door the owner of the house walked with him and said goodbye to him.

Before the man walked back to his house, something told him to look back and see the direction the old man was taking. When he looked the man had already disappeared. The Holy Spirit reminded him that Jesus had visited him.

He couldn't wait but just rushed straight to go and share with the other man to see if he had also seen Jesus. The other man told him how he waited and waited but no one came except this very old dirty man. Then he told him that that was Jesus who had visited him.

If pride is still ruling in us, however much we seek and call on God, when He comes we will still not know His visitation. If God tells you that he is going to do anything, you don't have to set the standards of who God should look like.

The way we conduct our lives has resisted the move of God breaking through in our churches. We only allow people with certain criteria to speak in our churches. Even when God sends his servants from afar, we sometimes judge them by their colour or background. We don't even stop and think that since God is not a respecter of persons, He can use any one for His glory.

I wish we would watch against the enemy like we watch against those who come in the name of God. Those that you despise are the very ones God is revealing Himself in because in that low profile they have set their hearts in the right position to meet God.

1 Corinthians 1:27
But God has chosen the foolish things of the world to put to shame the wise, and God has chosen the weak things of the world to put to shame the things which are mighty.

## It's Never Too Late

1 Peter 5:6-7
Therefore humble yourselves under the mighty hand of God that He may exalt you in due time. V7 casting all your care upon Him, for He cares for you.

We have seen how pride can rob us of God's blessings and rights. Thank God that even when Ishmael tried to take Isaac's rights, God wouldn't let it happen because He had already purposed Isaac to be a blessing.

God's plan for the church still stands because the church is in a blood covenant relationship with Him through Christ Jesus. He has promised the church that whatever belongs to Him belongs to her. That's why in the dream, I saw Jesus crying.

Jesus is still sitting on the right side of God pleading our cause. He says, 'My people I have placed you on the right side; you are mine. Whoever touches you touches the apple of my eye. Yes, Muslims may fight as much as they can to overpower you, but I will not let them, if you will only wake up and do according to my Father's will.

Before God comes to fulfil his Word, the enemy will always try to imitate or stop it. He can cause so many roadblocks in trying to obstruct people from receiving from God. But the Bible says, 'Whatever is born of God shall overcome the world'. Victory will come if we only humble ourselves under the guidance of the Holy Spirit.

The latter glory could not be revealed until the builders obeyed and went up the mountain to collect timber for rebuilding the house of God. God was willing to show Himself in the house, but He couldn't as long as the house was in a state of disrepair.

It was in a poor state because the foundations had been destroyed. The roof had been blown away by the wind. No one was caring for the house of God but everyone was building his own house and making a name for themselves.

Psalm 11:3
If the foundations are destroyed, what can the righteous do?

I picture the termites eating the pillars, cockroaches were infesting the temple because it had been abandoned. The Temple was falling because the pillars had become weak.

The former house was built on pride, division, hatred and other fleshly desires that it could not resist any wind. Because God had promised his servant Solomon that He was going to establish His house forever, He kept his word by asking all the concerned people, (just as He is asking His church to turn back to Him) to unite, everyone in his dignity and calling to go up the mountain to bring down timber to rebuild Him a house.

## Mountain Timber

Have you ever stopped yourself and wondered why specifically God instructed His people to use mountain timber instead of any timber they could land their eyes on? I am very sure that God singled out mountain timber for a specific reason. There must have been many other places where timber was grown and it was there in plenty.

There is a very big difference between mountain timber and other timber, let's say "city timber". City timber is man grown and it's grown for the beauty of the city but mountain timber is natural or organic.

The city timber grows quickly because of the fertilizers and the care it gets all the time, yet it is very soft. But the mountain timber takes longer to grow and endures strong winds and hard conditions that turns it into hard wood.

Brethren, time has come that it's not about how many courses we have done, but it's about the relationship with your God. We have seen many people who claim they have done this course and that one but they are as dry as a desert. There is no way you can relate them and their courses to their relationship with Christ.

Such people cannot build the kingdom of God but instead they are religion builders. These people are so eager to do what their religion tells them but not what God says. We also have another class of people who do courses because they want to teach others, not to hunger and thirst for God to change their lives. I mean there is nothing wrong with courses but above all, let Christ be the centre of all.

You see, when Jesus sent the twelve disciples, He told them to start from Judea, then Samaria and then to the whole world. The Judea Jesus talked about is that you yourself must be the centre or the starting point for the gospel of Jesus Christ. How will you tell your neighbours, the Samaritans, about Jesus when you haven't been changed yourself first?

You find people getting frustrated because they think God hasn't opened doors for them to preach. God says preach to yourself first and see if your testimony will not influence or impact those who come in contact with you, your workmates, your partner, your family.

For a very long time the Church of Christ has lived a city timber life that looks to be mature from the outside when inside is so soft that, they cannot even build a cubby house.

Did you know that the people we are looking at right now and see no beauty from the outside, are the ones that are mountain timbers. They may have not got the advantage of Bible Schools in their background and resume or they couldn't afford to go where you went but the little they know, they use to build their strong relationship with the Holy Spirit. They pray and fast and trusted Him to show them the great and unsearchable revelations like He said He would in his Word.

God is calling us to revisit his Word and allow it to mature our faith and righteousness as it has been purposed to do. It will mature us to be able to endure and overcome all the tribulations that come our way. God wants to rebuild His body so that will show His latter glory in the nations.

I look forward to those days when we will see Christians gathered in big stadiums of the cities worshipping God in one Spirit and heart. I look forward to the day when all men of God will plan everything with one heart without any one claiming that this is how we do our thing.

The former house was built under the influence of man but God is seeking to build His own house that will last forever; a house where the gates of hell shall not prevail. You and I, are the pillars that are going to rebuild the house of God. The churches in our cities are the ones that will constitute a house of God when they abide in strong unity and love.

## Self –Seeking

James 3:14 -16
But if you have bitter envy and self- seeking in your hearts, do not boast and lie against the truth. This wisdom does not descend from above, but is earthly, sensual, and demonic. For where envy and self - seeking exist, confusion and every evil thing are there.

Self-seeking people will never be certified by what others do. They always make sure they look for faults to get their own way. They don't want to be led or be under someone else. If they happen to be, then they want to be acknowledged as knowing more than others.

If such people come to a church and are not recognised, they begin to influence and mislead weak Christians. Their mission is moving from church to church recording the mistakes of the pastors, Christians and the method of worship. They don't sit back and consider why something was started, how and what it is the objective it is aiming at.

The Bible talks of a man who gave Moses a hard time from the time Moses started his deliverance ministry all the way through the wilderness. Even when God had done great miracles in the midst of all the Hebrews, Korah did not see that he was always trying to seek the disproval of Moses for people to start following him.

One time He challenged Moses as to why he thought God used him alone and where he got the power to lead. Moses was leading God's people to the Promised Land He gave to his servant Abraham but Korah was stirring up discontent in the Israelites. Why did Moses make them leave Egypt where at least they ate onions and water melons though they were continually under their task masters?

Self -seekers are there to sabotage the vision of Christ rather than supporting it. They will always want to gain at the expense of others.

In Egypt Korah was working in the king's palace so he couldn't care less as long as he and his family were living good lives. He preferred to remain in slavery for the sake of his position rather than proceeding to the total freedom that God had promised to take them to their own land. When he learned that Moses had come to deliver God's people, he opposed him because he knew if the people went, he would lose his position and end up just like anyone else. He didn't have a vision of the future, but he was quite happy with where he was even if he was known as a slave.

Self -seekers don't have dreams and don't see the future. They don't care where they stand spiritually with God as long as they achieve their wrong motives. They are willing to do anything to betray the church. They misinterpret the truth to others. They can be easily used by the enemy to turn against the work of God. The Bible says it is not that such people exist but woe unto them.

Matt 18:4

Woe to the world, because of offenses! For offenses must come, but woe to that man by whom the offense comes!

I want you to know that as you read this book, it's not designed to criticise or condemn any one.My desire and prayer is that we all realise the mistakes that are stopping us from experiencing the move of our God in our world.

Why is our enemy advancing against the Church? Jesus came with a good vision of reconciling us back to God, yet Judas didn't stop betraying him even when Jesus had loved him so much.

Jesus left people who would have been much better than Judas and He walked with him everywhere he went. Jesus loved him so much that he trusted him to be His treasurer but his selfish ambitions made him betray Jesus.

Friends, this example is not about how much Jesus loves us, but how we receive the love of Jesus. I have seen people who have stubbornly done things in the name of grace. People who don't want to change are good at condemning the law. They say we are no longer under the law for Christ has set us free by His grace.

When a friend gives you a beautiful gift and you abuse it by not looking after it, how do you think that makes him feel? Action speaks louder than words. If Christ has given us His grace and we abuse it, how do we think this is going to end up for us?

Judas had time to repent and change, but he decided to betray Grace and faced the consequences accordingly. You can do anything in the church today, backing your actions with Scriptures in your favour, but the fruit of your action will one day expose the error of your ways.

## Law and Grace

Before I got married, I got dreams of when my wedding day would arrive but I wasn't ready because my beauticians had not kept their appointment to get me ready. They had reluctantly refused to do so because they had prioritized other minor programs over me.

One of the dreams I had was, I was in this beautiful house and had all the beautiful preparations to get me ready for my wedding. Next to me was a small room in which there were two Muslim girls. They were also being prepared to get married to one man.

These two ladies didn't have anybody or anything to make themselves beautiful, yet they were inside the room all the time struggling to make themselves ready for their wedding day. So even though I had everything, I could not get inside the house, I just took things for granted. I decided to continue doing other things outside for I thought that there was still more time to get prepared.

I then saw my husband-to-be standing near me and crying bitterly and pleading with me to get inside my beautiful house. He sobbed and said to me, "Barbrah, I love you very much but you have refused to get yourself ready for me".

At that very time, I saw the Muslim girls, though they were getting married to one man, were in readiness, looking beautiful and very excited for their wedding day.

The dream ended without me being ready and my bride groom was so devastated.

Because of the same dreams I used to receive all the time, I prayed and asked God for the interpretation. The Lord said that they were not particularly meant for me but that I represented His church and the bridegroom represented Jesus Christ.

Eph 5:24-27
Therefore, just as the church is subject to Christ, so let the wives be to their own husbands in everything. Husbands love your wives, just as Christ also loved the church and gave Himself for her. That He might sanctify and cleanse her with the washing of water by the word. That He might present her to Himself a glorious church, not having spot or wrinkle or any such thing, but that she should be holy and without blemish.

The Holy Spirit told me that Muslims are faithfully doing everything in respect to their beliefs, however oppressive it is to them. They wash themselves and pray five times a day regarding their law but My church that I love so much is continually walking away from My grace.

My people have refused to get themselves ready for My coming, they think there is still time. My people are so unclean and unrepentant that even though they live sin, they still want to continue serving Me but do not care about cleaning and preparing themselves first.

When Muslims wash themselves five times a day, this is how they mentally ascend to their beliefs but my people are unclean before me.

God doesn't work with self -seekers but he works with those of self-denial. The Bible says that the cost of being a disciple is to carry your own cross and follow Jesus. Many have Christ, but not many follow him. They claim to love Jesus, but are in fact, enemies of the cross of Christ.

Philippians 3:18
(For many walk, of whom I have told you often, and now tell you even weeping, that they are the enemies of the cross of Christ:

How many people have walked away from Christ, because he has not given them what they thought He should give them? How many people have asked you more than five times to give them something? But every time they approached you, you said, "No, or wait." As a result they resent you? Many people resent Christ for not answering their prayers. I think the hour is here when we are required to serve Christ for the love He gives us not for the things He is going to do for us.

Matt 6:33
But seek first the kingdom of God and his righteousness, and all these things shall be added to you.

## Who is Leading You to the Promised Land?

Many people have exalted themselves into leadership roles. But remember, it is God who chooses leaders. A true leader is known by his fruits.

Moses didn't go around the Israelite camp campaigning to be voted in as their leader. The spirit in him would not allow him to enjoy the pleasures of the palace when his people were suffering. The leadership spirit in him humbled him to go and labour with his people after he realised that he was in the wrong family that on the surface felt to be right for him.

Far from what he originally thought, he finally walked away from all the troubles of Egypt to start his own family and conduct a simple task of looking after his father-in-law's cattle, where God called him to lead his people. I said earlier that David was tending his father's flock before he was anointed a King of Israel.

In Africa, a person who tends other people's flocks is the most disadvantaged and very lowly esteemed person on the continent. He has no power to choose a different occupation but does shepherding work for survival. He can't save or buy anything from the income he earns.

You see, here the call of leadership, takes Moses from being a prince to a shepherd. True leaders humble themselves in order that God Himself would raise them up to lead His people in humility. Moses went back to Egypt to lead God's people irrespective of the dangers that might be expected ahead.

Today we have leaders who qualify themselves by degrees but are not willing to stand with people to assist with the bondages in their lives. They are leaders who only want perfect people in their churches and if they hear anything about a Christian who has had a sordid past they ask him or her to leave their churches.

God help us! Where do we get the authority to cast people out of churches when Christ is welcoming them to come as they are? It makes me wonder whether people are leading Christ's church or their own businesses. Why are we not willing to go through everything with them until we bring them to their victory?

In the church I pastored in Uganda, there was a young man who was a known robber and was wanted by the police. He had been involved in so many crimes that even his own father offered money for someone to kill him. He used to live in the bush and isolated places in fear for his life.

One day I was at home sitting under a tree during day time and I saw him walking to me in tears. He said, "Pastor Barbrah, I have sat down and thought and I have realised that no one loves me including my parents. My life is messed up and I may die anytime soon, but I don't want to die and go to hell." He said, "I have come to you because I know your God can forgive and save me".

Every word he said felt like a knife cutting through my heart and left me in tears. I noticed that he was tired of the way he had lived his life. He was carrying rejection in him and there was no way he could get out of this state as he was completely bound.

He said pastor, "If you also say no to me then I will go and hang myself. I have suffered a lot in this world".

I agreed to pray for him and lead him through the sinner's prayer to give his life to Christ. One thing I noticed after praying for him was, hope and happiness were restored to him instantly.

When he started coming to church and people saw him with me, they criticised me and said "you are the one encouraging thieves in our community. Why are you keeping this boy among the young children?" People stood against me with all sorts of accusations but I said to God nothing is impossible with you. You sent your son Jesus to die for sinners. He one time wrote in the dust and all the accusers of an adulterous woman walked away. I said Lord you are the only one who knew what you wrote that dispersed her accusers. Would you please write something in the dust on behalf of this boy for many to walk away from him?

I took the boy as my own son and discipled him amidst the persecution. Some people decreed to kill me if the boy did anything bad to anyone, but I said, "Lord, I would rather die doing the right thing by you." God filled my heart with a lot of love and compassion for this boy to 'be there' for him. He became a very strong believer in the faith of our Lord and after everything he had been through, God used him to change many lives. Nothing is too hard for the blood of Jesus.

Sometimes we have to risk going beyond our reach to rescue God's people. You see, we have to know that if those people were able to help themselves then there would be no need of God calling us to serve Him. Jesus said, "The Spirit of God is upon me for He has sent me to set free the captives and the opening of the prisoners". You cannot free a prisoner unless you go into the prison. You cannot free the bound unless you put your hands to work to break the chains. If we knew how to free ourselves Jesus would have not needed to come.

God wants the church to take responsibility for her leadership role until governments send criminals to them for rehabilitation before they return to the community. We hear people complaining about the justice system that has failed them. In reality, it's the church that has failed the communities. We are so involved running after other things and have left the real reason for our existence.

As leaders, we need to reach out to people with open arms who have been sidelined due to their past. We need to love them so they see the light of God. When they come to us, if they are meant to stay, they will change, but if not they will go. We don't need to chase them.

We should know that not everyone is called to lead us into God's promises. However, all of us are called to enter the Promised Land. The mistake that some people make, is when God promises something, they don't trust Him to show them where and how His promise will come to pass. Instead, they rush ahead and try to make things work out for themselves.

Today we have many leaders who are struggling to make decisions yet they are supposed to lead others into their promises. My concern is that if everyone is struggling to be a leader, who is going to be a follower.

I imagine that when Moses came and told the Israelites that he was leading them to the Promised Land, everyone became so excited and was looking forward to getting to the land flowing with milk and honey. That's why you see people like Joshua, irrespective of what they went through in the wilderness, they kept on encouraging themselves through Moses vision until they reached the Promised Land. They were willing to be led even if they themselves were called to lead.

Hosea 4:6
My people are destroyed for lack of knowledge. Because you have rejected knowledge, I also will reject you from being priests for me. Because you have forgotten the law of your God, I also will forget your children.

Earlier on, I said to be a priest meant you have access to communicating with God and know His plans. Whenever God gives us His promises and we lose the understanding of them, He rejects us and assigns us to continue doing what we think we know.

In the entire Christian community, especially the Pentecostals, there is a belief that if everyone wants to succeed in his/her dream he must start his own church.

It was challenging for me when I came to Australia. God had promised me that Australia was going to be my Promised Land. When I arrived, everyone back home expected me to start a church in order to prosper.

But as I said, starting churches is not my call. I came from being a great leader, to a humble follower in other ministries. So people, who knew me back home, and those who heard me speak, whenever they came and saw me just sitting in the pew, they got worried that I might lose the fire and my vision.

They didn't have any idea that God had brought me from being a great leader to a follower, to be led into my promises. Since I wasn't familiar with the Australian culture, God had prepared a Moses to lead me into my destiny. Therefore for Moses to lead me I had to serve under him and listen to his instructions.

There are so many things that the men and women of God in Australia have helped me to achieve that I would have not received, if I had started my own ministry.

Who lied to us that success is into starting our own fellowship of believers? Let me tell you, you will never become a Joshua unless you work for Moses. You will never become Elisha unless you work for

Elijah. Why? Because Moses knows where you came from and where you are going. He knew where you were going before you started on your journey.

You see, people looked at me and thought I was finished but I tell you, I was instead refuelling myself for the great work ahead of me in Australia and the nations.

## The Source of Money

Some people can't afford to serve under others because they think that by doing so, they will never achieve their goals. That's why today the church is looked on as a business.

I want us to think about this, if everyone had a furniture store or grocery shop, where do you think, the customers would come from. Don't we see that there will be an excess of supply over demand and products will sit rotting in stores that will cause competition.

Did you know that by everyone wanting to be a leader has caused a lot of competition and jealousy in the body of Christ?

Assuredly I tell you that if God has never called you to be a leader, even if you train with leadership skills, you will only be a professional leader but you will never manage to lead in the things of God. If God has never called you to be a leader and you force yourself, you will either be a dictator or a weak leader. True leadership of God is achieved by His grace and Spirit.

If God has appointed you to be a leader in His church, He will give you the required wisdom, favour and grace before people. They will listen to and believe in you, even if you are not professional because they see something in you that brings them closer to God.

Many Christians are in the wilderness today because they wanted to form their own fellowships like Korah, or they were influenced by the Korah governments.

Moses and Korah were both leaders, but the difference was that Korah was a leader in the land of bondage, whereas Moses was a leader to the Promised Land. Korah was a rebellious leader but Moses was leading a royal priesthood, a chosen generation and a holy nation to God.

True leaders have got a passion to bring people closer to God. They actually lead the way to God and others follow. People are sick of leaders who speak the word, but their lives are not in right standing with God.

If you are under such people, you had better pray to God to show the true leader who will save you from perishing in the wilderness. You didn't leave Egypt to perish on the way, but to enter the Promised Land.

Today we have thousands of leaders but few godly leaders. I didn't write this to disorganise churches. But am saying to you, if you were planning to go and start your own church because you feel you have an anointing, stay where you are and wait for God to use you mightily.

You can only move when God Himself says so. You might be a leader, but God has not called you in the same position and work as he called Moses. Position yourself and you will understand what kind/level of a leader you are meant to be.

The church of Christ needs all levels and kinds of leadership to function. Churches are lacking leadership teams because people have decided to go and do their own things.

You find a pastor is struggling to do everything because of imbalanced leadership. Please realise your position so that Moses maybe free to go up the mountain and spend more time with God to lead you to the land of milk and honey. As soon as we get there, we will occupy it and prosper in everything we do.

God wants to raise up millionaires in the church. Why not? He wants to raise great leaders from the church to take back governments and businesses for Christ. He says he has not only called us to be leaders of small congregations. He has called us to be leaders of great companies. It is time for some of you people to take the advantage of being in the church to think and dream larger and wider than the four corners of a church.

God doesn't want to see his children struggling with His work all the time. He wants to see us enjoy the earth and its goodness. A church is meant to be a place of acquiring God's wisdom and plans to go and display them outside. The enemy has robbed us of these positions due to narrow mindedness.

The whole of Exodus chapter 18 tells how Moses was overloaded with work until his father-in-law advised him to choose leaders and leaders of leaders, thereby delegating responsibilities and relative authority.

1 Corinthians 12:27-28
Now you are the body of Christ and members individually. And God has appointed these in the church. First apostles, second prophets, third teachers, after that miracles, then gifts of healing, helps, administrations, varieties of tongues.

## The Fear of God

Ps 111:10
The fear of the Lord is the beginning of wisdom; a good understanding have all those who do His commandments. His praise endures forever.

Wisdom and fear are one, just as the Father and the Son are one. We cannot expect to walk in the wisdom of God without his fear. The fear of God is exercised in keeping His word or commandment. For example, He says 'obey your parents that all may go well with you'.

When I say parents, I mean both biological and spiritual parents. Spiritual parents are the people who introduce us to the Lord and then help us to grow in the things of God. Pastors for example.

Before God said we should respect our parents, He knew there would be some who would be abusive to their children. God didn't give the commandment based on the negative side of parents, as every man has weaknesses. He based it on the positive things we inherit from them.

Having a good relationship with our parents gives us the opportunity of avoiding making same mistakes they made. It guides us to learn from their experiences as well. Either way, we can build from their achievements and failures. You can use their challenges of failure to build yourself a better road to success.

God is a Father. When He puts more emphasis on children obeying their parents, He knows what can be achieved when they do so. A parent may be in the position where it's too late to change but as a child you still have many opportunities to define yourself. Once we start counting the disappointments of our parents, then that also is the beginning of our failures. Failure will then influence us to walk out their lives in disobedience, which in turn, results in curses rather than parental blessings.

I tell you there is a blessing that God has bestowed on every parent whether they are either good or bad. There is no parent who wishes their children to fail, unless that parent has psychological problems. Every parent wants the best for their children.
Proverbs 10:1
A wise son brings honour to his father but a foolish one brings sorrow to the mother.

As children, we have no right for judging or persecuting our parents. God Himself alone has that responsibility. There are so many people who have walked out of churches because they felt those churches were not doing the right thing by God. Not only that, they spread bad words against their leaders.

You see, Noah did the wrong thing by stripping himself naked. The son who laughed and went to call others was cursed and the ones who didn't want to look at their father's nakedness were blessed for covering him.

If you find yourself in a situation like that it is good to turn to God and ask Him to tell you what to do, with the exception of using your parent's wickedness to establish yourself.

Look at Absalom, David's son, who tried to use his father's wickedness to take over his kingdom. Though it was hurtful for David as a father to see his son killed, God Himself had passed judgment against him.

I have seen many churches stand over a period of time even though people believed that those churches they were not good. True, they may not have been preaching the truth, but at least, thank God, He used them to introduce you to the knowledge of God's word in which you have discovered the truth.

Instead of using that as reason enough to leave your church, why don't you use the truth to elevate them to your level. After you have stood the test of time, help others.

We spend years moving from church to church, recycling time after time, instead of maturing the church we are in to overcome hell's gates. Most of us are recycled Christians instead of restored ones.

The difference between the two is that recycling is the practice of reusing items that would otherwise be discarded as waste. But restoration is the act or process of returning something to its original condition or beauty by repairing it, cleaning it, etc.

I believe God is saying to us that the time to recycle churches is over and now is the time to restore His church to His original plan.

There was an incident in Uganda in the nineteen eighties, where one minister had a fight with his father. He said to his father, "A person like you, when will you ever get the opportunity to be a minister like me?" The father answered, "When will you ever be a proud father, whose son is a minister of the status like me with that attitude of yours?"

The father then said, "Son, I may never be a minister but at least I have seen the product of being a good father. I can count my achievements. What about you?"

Proverbs 13:1
A wise son heeds his father's instruction but a scoffer does not listen to rebuke.

People may not like the idea of Isaac re-digging the wells of his father Abraham because they gave him nothing but trouble until he decided to dig his own.

There is also a good side to the story. To me, I believe he wanted to follow his father's footsteps to discover what his father's source of failures and successes were in his journey. By following them, he got to know his father's enemies, being aware of them.

I told you about my pastor's story before. There came a time when he also made mistakes like anybody else. During that time some people walked away in criticism and judgment against him. For me, as a young, vibrant preacher, I began to pray and ask God what could be done in this situation.

One time, praying, the Lord Himself told me, "I am sending you back to your homeland to go and start afresh." I loved and respected my pastor so much that when I came home, I told him what the Lord had asked me to do and he blessed me. After I had started the work I faced a lot of opposition from other people but not from my pastor. He was always there for me and was so supportive in the ministry. As we continued working together, God spoke to him and some members of his church to come and join us if they wanted to prosper.

As the pastor began operating in his call of evangelism, God began opening doors for him that everywhere he went he witnessed souls coming to Christ and God's favour and grace was upon him.

Now the fact that God asked him to surrender and come under me, an instruction which is still a big challenge for most people, didn't mean he was not my spiritual father. He was so proud of me that wherever he went, he talked a lot about me.

Through him, God opened more doors for me, I began getting invitations from people I didn't know saying the pastor told them about me. You see, God raises us to become a blessing not a disgrace to our parents. He blesses us to be a blessing to those who bless us.

Instead of wasting our time talking about what others don't do, let's do what we can so that God may use us to make them also do what we are doing. The enemy has got such a hold in this area, the former churches can't understand what the latter churches are doing. And the latter churches are criticising what the former churches didn't do. So as the two churches rub against each other, he prints the bad news about the church for the readers.

As a church we will not be judged for committing sin but for failing to represent the image of God in our communities. Our behaviours have blocked many from entering the kingdom of God. It's time we examined ourselves and mend our ways. It's time to rebuild the broken bridges to allow the flow of God's move to touch His people.

## The Blessing of Esau and the Blessing of Jacob

Please read the whole chapter of Genesis 27 to get the complete story. I will emphasise verses 27-29 when Isaac blessed Jacob and 38-40.

V27 Then his father Isaac said to him, come near now and kiss me, my son. He smelled the smell of his clothing and blessed him and said, surely the smell of my son is like the smell of a field which the Lord has blessed.

V28.Therefore, may God give you of the dew of heaven of the fatness of the earth, and plenty of grain and wine.

V29 let peoples serve you, and nations bow down to you. Be master over your brethren, and let your mother's sons bow down to you. Cursed be everyone who curses you

Esau's v38 And Esau said to his father, "have you only one blessing, my father? Bless me – me also, my father!!"And Esau lifted up his voice and wept.

V39 Then Isaac his father answered and said to him

"Behold your dwelling shall be of the fatness of the earth, and of the dew of heaven from above.

V40 By your sword you shall live, and you shall serve your brother, and it shall come to pass, when you become restless, that you shall break his yoke from your neck.

The two brothers were both blessed with the same blessing – in verse 28 and verse 39.However Esau's blessing was through much pain and tears. It wasn't given to him from the father's heart but was a replica of the original blessing passed to Jacob. Jacob was blessed with a generational right that was passed down from his grandfather for obeying the Lord God. It was a royal blessing that determined ones authority and power.

Royals don't work for respect and honour. All these things have been included for them and they are provided the instant they are conceived in their mother's womb. Royals are not voted into power because power is part of their inheritance.

Jeremiah 1:5
Before I formed you in the womb I knew you. I ordained you a prophet to the nations.

Prophets have the same authority as kings; they speak under the authority of King Jesus.

Today most people operate under the common blessing of Esau and Ishmael rather than the original blessing of King Jesus. The blessing of Esau and Ishmael makes a great nation yet the individual is powerless in the things of God. The power is derived from much struggling and suffering. When most people receive this blessing, they stop seeking God's internal blessings.

For example, what the church calls a blessing is when someone has a lot of money. But what about those wealthy people who don't know God? At least there has been a blessing that makes us different from others. It was this blessing that was worthy of Jacob forsaking everything out-doors in order to have it. It was the blessing that gave him access in wrestling with the angel who changed his name from Jacob to Israel. As a result of changing his name, he received the revelation that he was sleeping in the presence of God. This was more than his head simply resting on a rock.

The blessing of Israel brings us closer to God for us to name our world instead of us just being named.

The blessing I am talking about is the one that the devil is willing to give us everything to hinder us from receiving it. It's the blessing of inheriting and being heirs with Jesus in the kingdom of God.

Mathew 4:9
And He said to Him, all these things I will give you if you will fall down and worship me.

The devil was originally a servant in heaven and he knows the glory that the heirs to the kingdom throne live in. It's this very kingdom that brought his downfall by him trying to overtake it. Therefore, he is out to try anything to prevent the church of Christ from being called royals and walking in royal benefits.

Children of God, we are so honoured by our God that we didn't have to do anything to qualify to have His kingdom. It actually cost the priceless life of the Son of God for us to become kings and priests.

Despite what it cost Jesus for us to achieve this position, I have seen people trade away their rights in order to gain worldly pleasures.

There was a time in Uganda when there was a belief that everyone who travelled to America was blessed by God. People would fast and pray believing God to send them to America so that when they returned they would speak English with an American accent. Everyone would acknowledge them as anointed and blessed by God.

I remember when going to every church and meeting I could hear pastors prophesying people to America. They used to prophesy the aeroplane was waiting for us and we were going to get a lot of money. During this time, Christians were not focusing on making their ways right with God but everyone was trusting God to go to America to get money.

These prophecies would leave me wondering about the ungodly people who go to America. Who gives them the blessing? I also used to wonder whether all Americans are God fearing. I always knew there has to be something different and more valuable than going to America, having money and speaking American English.

Many servants of God have been deceived into thinking that if they have lots of money, then God's presence is with them even though they are involved in ungodly activities.

You know, if the enemy wants you to serve him, he can give you all the money you need to do anything.

We have to be able to discern between the blessings from God and the enemy's counterfeit. God's blessings are bestowed as a result of humbling ourselves and seeking Him first. It is good to have money when you know it didn't cost you your inheritance and rights.

I am one of those who celebrate when I see men and women of God living luxurious lives. I have no problem with that. That kind of life comes in the package of kingship blessings. Kings and queens have the best of the best, we all need that life.

I see people complaining on how servants of God aren't supposed to live the best life. I always ask some people, who are the people meant for the best life?

Instead of counting how much the servants of God waste, why can't we count what government leaders waste? They are ministers and representatives of the governments; we are ministers and representatives of the Heavenly kingdom.

The enemy has got the church focused on money when it should be concentrated on her inheritance in God. God wants the church to operate in the same authority and power like Him. He is not interested in having powerless and voiceless churches in the communities. He wants the church to be the solution to a dying world, a place of refuge where people turn after trying everything else that has failed. He wants His church to lead in every way, not just have people who speak a lot but have no substance seen in them. An empty tin makes a lot of noise. We are very busy travelling and speaking all the time without the production of the fruit of the Spirit. This is why the enemy has the church where it is because he knows the church 'barks but doesn't bite'.

Matt 28:18-19

And Jesus came and spoke to them, saying all authority has been given to me in heaven and on earth. Go therefore and make disciples of all the nations, baptizing them in the name of the father and of the Son and of the Holy Spirit.

God wants the church to take her stand in the kingship status. This is the same kind of inheritance that Muslims are fighting for. They want the whole world to become Muslim in order that they may rule.

Muslims are not fighting for money because they already have it. They are using money to fight and divert many to their beliefs.

Christians, let's rise up and stand for our rights by spending time in His presence and doing what it takes to fulfil the Great Commission. When we secure the blessing of God in verses 27 & 29 then verse 28 and 39 will follow us. We don't want to leave in verse 40 where we have to fight and struggle all the time working hard to make others rich because we are their servants.

# CHAPTER FOUR

## MONEY

The highest percentage of Christians engage themselves in prayer only when they are in need. But once their needs are met, the desire to seek God recedes. Money has dominated the voice of God instead of being the other way round.

When God asks us to do things, we first think of where we will get money from. So instead of seeking God to bring money, we seek money to do God's assignments. God cannot assign you and fail to sign the cheques.

There was a time when I was on the bank of the source of river Nile praying in Jinja district. I felt so distressed in my spirit that I began to cry. The Holy Spirit spoke to me and said, "I have so much wanted to use this nation of Uganda for my glory but my people can't do without money". My response to Him was, "Lord give me another chance and send me".

I believe that God spoke to me about Uganda, because it was the only nation I was in at the time. I believe this message applies to the whole church of Christ.

I am not saying that Christians don't need money but we shouldn't love it over our God. We shouldn't allow money to dictate our loyalty to God, for the God we have is greater than the money we need. He wants us to serve him with or without it. God doesn't want us to trade His word for money. He says freely you have received, therefore freely give.

God clearly promises to bless us wherever we go in His name. He said he will neither leave us nor forsake us. He who gives the vision will provide for the vision to be accomplished. He who gives the ministry will administer the ministry. We don't have to limit God and put conditions on Him.

The devil uses money to control people in sin, but God uses His Spirit to inspire His people into total freedom and abundance.

I have so many testimonies of how I have seen God reward me in different places where I have ministered.

One time my sister and I went from Uganda to Kenya to pray for a certain family that had been possessed by demons for many years. The head of the family invited us but he never provided any transport. We had to use our own means to get there and back, yet he was financially well off.

We didn't know whether it was God testing us through him to see whether we would complain or not. We had spent four days in the room praying and fasting for them while they ate.

We prayed until God spoke to us that he had delivered the family. Before we left their son and daughter who were asthmatics, were healed and began to eat. The children were rushed to the hospital almost every second day. The mother had

had enough to the extent that she wanted them to die rather than continue to see them suffer. Besides that, the only reward he gave us was a short ride to the bus station.

God was still testing us. After the news spread around of what God had done, on Sunday we were invited to a nearby church to preach. Many people came to the church to be prayed for and give their lives to Christ. God's power was so strong, even the people walking by came crying, wanting to give their lives to the Lord.

After everything that God had used us to do, the pastor never gave us anything, even though the church wasn't poor. It was a big church in the city.

Nevertheless, all our excitement was focused on what we had seen God do through us. It is a good feeling to see God working through you and to see people just cry for salvation.

Now it happened that in the final moments, we received a phone call from one of our friends. He was a prominent person in the government of Kenya. He had gone home to see us but was told where we were and was given the telephone number to call.

The ways of God are very different and interesting when we walk in them. When our friend phoned he requested us not to return to Uganda, before first going to his place.

Our God is so faithful and rewards openly. When we arrived at his place, God had spoken to him to bless us with a good amount of money. It was like God went before us when we went to do His work. He had already prepared a package for us from somewhere else. The money he gave us was the first time I handled such a large amount. I guess it was more than what we would have gotten from both the family and church if we had put our focus on them. When you serve God in anyway, strive to see that you impress God who has such a big heart, before anybody else.

From that time I learned that sometimes when we serve God and expect compensation from people, we limit ourselves, but when we look unto God He rewards us with abundance.

You see, when God uses a different channel to reward you, it builds your confidence and faith to know that God is pleased with you. For me, when I go to churches to minister, I don't care whether I am given a love offering or not. As long as God's people are blessed, I am happy. My joy is in seeing God's people transformed and by that I gain more rewards in my account in Heaven.

People could come to me and ask where I get the money to do all the things I do. The secret is being loyal and obedient to the voice of God. When God tells me to do things, I don't try and figure out what I should say or do to impress or convince people to give, but I trust Him who asks me to do His will, and He consequently provides in various ways.

Ecclesiastes 11:1
Cast your bread upon many waters, for you will find it after many days.

V2 Give a serving to seven and also to eight. For you do not know what evil will be on the earth.

Deuteronomy 28:1

Now it shall come to pass if you diligently obey the voice of the Lord your God, to observe carefully all his commands which I command you today that the Lord your God will set you high above all nations of the earth.

V2 And all these blessings shall come upon you and overtake you, because you obey the voice of the Lord your God.

## Casting Your Bread upon Many Waters

Psalm 29:3
The voice of the LORD is over the waters
The God of glory thunders:
The Lord is over many waters
The voice of the LORD is powerful;
The voice of the LORD is full of Majesty.

I like using everyday life situations to relate to what the Scriptures say. When the Scripture says to cast the bread, it does not mean casting in small creeks or rivers but in the ocean because this is the only place that has many waters.

The bread you are being asked to throw might be a loaf or even a few slices that are enough for you. Think about what is just enough for you. It might be something that God instructed you to do.

When Jesus taught His disciples how to pray, He told them to pray for God to give them their daily bread. The bread was not meant to be stored in the pantries or fridges. They were to eat what was enough for the day and cast the excess into the great waters.

Listen, God doesn't give us bread to store it. However, where we cast it matters a lot. The Scripture has directed us to where exactly we are to cast our bread.

You see, some people fail to cast their bread because they see the ocean of real life as being impossible to reward them, so they decide to keep their bread.

I want us to just think of a picture of the ocean and everything in it. It covers the whole world. When you cast your pieces of bread from Australia or anywhere, you don't necessarily have to know which side of the world it will appear from.

The ocean is full of bread lovers everywhere, for example, fish. In actual life you can't cast bread in the water and see it last for a minute. It will become soggy and sea creatures will appear to fight over it.

The Scripture doesn't promise us to find the increase after only a few seconds but it says after many days. One day in the presence of God is like a thousand years. So as well, know that the timing for you to find your bread lies with God Himself. It's only your faith in the word of God that can preserve your bread and cause it to float on the water without being destroyed or eaten.

Did you know that when God calls you and gives you the word to take to the nations that word floats upon many waters? When He sends you, He wants you to have great faith like the ocean and wait on Him to provide for you. The bread itself is the word of God that is upon many waters and it is like many waters.

God also wants us to cast our bread when we give. When you give, don't expect a return from where you have given. Don't look at how much you have given but look at what you are required to give. Let our giving be unconditional, for in this, we will see God move on our behalf.

The people, who preach and expect to get support from the place where they ministered, are like those who cast their bread, and after a short time remove it.

The longer you let your bread float on the water days and nights, enter in and out of different time zones, move over distances and survive predators, the more preserved and tastier it will be.

I cast my bread in Uganda and I found it in Australia. Even when I arrived in Australia I never stopped casting my bread. I have never ceased praying. I have never stopped giving and I have never stopped trusting God for the provision of everything. Jesus didn't instruct the disciples to ask once, but He told them to ask every day.

There are some people God has raised to higher places and in the process have forgotten to cast their bread. They look at the abundance they currently find themselves in and see no need to cast. Asking God for provision is an everyday requirement and He will never scorn you for doing that. Once we stop casting, then we are going to survive on second best, not the fresh blessings from God.

Once we remove our focus from God and start looking to people, we will fail. There are some stubborn Christians in churches who don't want to change and as long as they give or support any project, they consider they have met the requirement. They make the priests of God sanction offering lame animals? They have put their treasures where their hearts are not because they give with wrong motives and think they can bribe God to bestow His righteousness.

I have learned to do what I am required to do and let my God provide my needs. My passion is in serving the Lord. I want to see people saved and transformed so much that God would call me a faithful servant and reward me with all His blessings.

## Everyone Needs Money

This particular part of the dream, "everyone wants money", captured my attention and made me sad to see that Christians had lost the original purpose of God. They were using His favour to achieve their own selfish motives.

The Bible talks of two sons who were assigned responsibilities by their father before he went away. The first son refused at first but when the father returned, he had fulfilled his assignment. The second son accepted the assignment but when the father returned, he had not done anything.

Christians are adept at humbling themselves at the feet of Jesus, desperately crying for Him to use us. We find it very easy to ask God to use us in any way He wants but when the responsibility arises that requires our attention, we discard it completely. Our commitment to God is only words, our hearts are not in it.

People we look at and think are ungodly, often respond to any need whole heartedly without asking questions. Jesus is not going to reward us for simply accepting Him but He will base our reward on our obedience to His will.

When the father returned he rewarded his first son for realising his mistake and judged the second for walking away from his word. The Bible tells us that the first shall be last and the last shall be first.

You may abuse God's favour in your life now, but the time will soon come when the favour will be transferred to those people, you see practising evil. They will turn back to God because of their generous hearts.

We are not saved by works but we can find a Saviour through works. Read the whole of Acts 10, you will get my point. It talks about Cornelius who was God fearing, gave generously to the people and prayed but was not saved. Through his faithful works the angel of God appeared to him and sent Peter to come and pray for him and his household's salvation.

In the dream everyone was using God's purposes to accumulate wealth for their own little kingdoms. The Bible tells us to invest our wealth in the kingdom of God, where no moth, rust or robber can break in.

I will tell you where I think Christians have lost the intended focus of giving. We give to our own ministry networks that have agreed to be under our authority. We have ceased to trust the Holy spirit to guide us and show us where and to whom to be a blessing.

We give with attached strings and conditions because we want others to do things our way not their way.

Personally, I don't want someone to give me something and then put me under pressure, demanding to know what I did with the gift. I don't call that a blessing from God. If the same God trusts you to bless me, why can't He also trust me to use the gift for the intended purposes?

The issue of dictatorial people has misled many into deception before God because they seek to please men. Don't we think if we give people the freedom to allow the Holy Spirit guide them, He will attract God's blessing for all of us?

What about if you give to me and the Lord asks me to give what you have given to someone else? Sometimes God's blessings can just pass through our hands when they are intended for someone else. We have to be very sensitive to the will of the Holy Spirit. It has happened to me many times and it can be very hard to let go.

One time I didn't need to buy shoes but as I was walking past the shoe shop, my eyes went straight to a particular coloured pair of shoes. They were the only unique shoes in the shop. I felt my spirit leading me to buy them.

When I got home, I lost the desire to wear them so I just set them aside. After a very long time, one Sunday morning I felt so strongly in my heart to wear the shoes. As I was walking through the door of the church, my eyes went straight to a lady who was wearing the same coloured dress as my shoes.

The Holy Spirit said to me, "these shoes belong to her". I somehow tried to ignore the voice but as I sat down the conviction made me unsettled and became stronger. I could hear the same words, 'those shoes belong to that lady'.

As I finally got to the pulpit to preach, I looked at the lady, who was also looking at my shoes and following my movements. I could see in her eyes how she really admired those shoes. At that moment I called her and gave the shoes to her.

She burst into tears saying, she had bought her dress but couldn't afford to buy the matching shoes but she decided to keep it. In the morning, while she was preparing to come to church, she felt divided in wearing the dress. When she saw me wearing my shoes, God spoke to her that the shoes belonged to her. But because she wasn't sure whether it was God or not, she made a vow to God that if she got the shoes she would also give her wall clock to the church.

What happened in this story may not seem to have a lot of meaning but how God worked in it, is so phenomenal. When I asked her how long she had kept the dress, it turned out that she bought it the same time I bought the shoes.

Many times, we find ourselves disappointed in vain, when we don't let God use us the way He wills. We are only human beings who can't afford to meet people's needs unless God works through us.

I have seen many Christians judging others to be liars for not doing what they wanted them to do, not what God required. I am saying this because there was a situation in Africa one time. A servant of God came to one family and while he was there, he felt God telling him to bless the family with some money.

Now when he gave them the money, he told them what to do with it. After he left, the family thought to themselves and decided that what he had offered them was not their urgent need. They used the money to buy something they had trusted God for a very long time.

When they told him about their decision, he called them liars and thieves who stole from him. I don't know whether he understood who the thief was. They did not force him or take the money out of his pocket by force but God simply used him to answer the family's prayer.

In the fact that the family didn't do as he said, he called them thieves. He even said God was going to punish the family for being unfaithful to him. Such incidents have occurred a lot and have made others appear to look unfaithful to God when they are not. I believe it would have been better if the servant had asked the family what they wanted first.

We see in some places, Jesus would ask people what they wanted first before He would minister to them. Do we think Jesus didn't know about these people's needs? He would give someone a miracle to walk yet his point of need was to be free from demons.

For example the blind man called on him at the roadside. The man was a total destitute who had a lot to work on in order to bring his life back to normal. When Jesus turned to him, I am sure He noticed additional problems but He focused on the man's major need.

We see the man requested his sight for he knew that it was the cause of all other disabilities. He wanted his sight back to recirculate in society, start looking for work and get a family to provide for.

God has called us to rectify the problem, not just control it. Anything controlled can run out of control. If God is going to use us to change the nations, we have to be willing to serve people at the point of their needs not what we think they want.

Phillipians4:19
And my God shall supply all my need according to His riches in glory by Christ Jesus.

I believe the big basket I saw in the dream was the basket of offerings for others' needs (Malachi 3:10).Muslims are so generous in the way that even the poor people in the streets look forward to their days of worship.

On Friday you find very many disadvantaged people gathered around the entrances of mosques waiting for the believers to give them money. During the month of fasting, Muslims walk on the streets giving away food and money to strangers.

Their belief is that they don't have to know someone before they give to them, but they should generously continue giving because at any time they may be giving to an angel. They have love and unity for fellow Muslims regardless of which group someone belongs to. Their connection is instant and genuine unlike Christians.

When you attack an individual Muslim, which means "Brethren", you are considered to have attacked the whole religion. I used to see at school when you fight any one of them, that because of their faith, you would trigger all the Moslems in the school to hunt for you even though they didn't know each other.

## Fighting for One Another

Christians, the Bible forbids us fighting against flesh and blood but how many times have we fought for one another even though we are not in the same church? Talking about fighting, I mean mental, emotional, financial and other battles we face.

Christians are their own worst enemies of Christianity. Once we hear or see other churches that don't belong to us going through tough times, we promote negativity about them instead of fighting for them through prayer.

We like to see them fall so that their members may join our churches or would like take over their buildings. We have to learn to think beyond our four-square boxes, for God has called us all with His love and the same cause.

One time I got shocked at hearing a servant of God addressing his church to pray that God would perform a miracle for him so that he could take over the premises of another church that was experiencing troubles.

It was like wanting your brother to die and take over his wife and belongings instead of taking him to the hospital. I believe it's time for us to reconsider the way we serve in the things of God. It's beyond me how we have allowed the devil to deceive us through the names of our ministries to think that we are any different from others. God wants us to be cheerful givers, even more than Moslems.

When we give in faith we also reap in faith. Moslems are very faithful givers.This is what I saw when even the poor were also striving to put at least something in their basket. That's how it is in real life, Muslims give a lot and that's why they prosper a lot also.

## Giving by Faith

In all my time of walking with the Lord, I have been one of those who gives by faith. Because of that, I have always found myself in the position where I can trust God for money to do something and He brings the manifestation in an expected way.

Basically, when God called me, one of the things I asked him was that He would never allow me to beg. I will tell you why I hate begging later on. God heard my prayers and promised to be my source of supply if I would rely on Him. He clearly spoke to me in the dream: "Barbrah, don't trust in missions but always look to Me", while He was pointing to heaven. How God blesses me sometimes is so amazing. I may have some money that is the same amount of money someone somewhere is praying and trusting God for. As I pray and remind God of his promises, He tells me to give the money to that person. I don't need to necessarily have any ministry relationship with that person. I may have seen them once in a church or somewhere but God knows everyone's needs.

After doing the will of God and telling that person about it, he is amazed and thanks God for answering his prayer. Then tells me that I have given exactly the amount he/she was trusting God for.

I have also realised that, whenever God uses us in this way, it is when someone maybe desperately in need.

For example, few years ago we were praying and trusting God to get us enough money to go to Uganda. He had told us to dedicate our son to Him in our Church in Uganda.

He had instructed us to do many things but we didn't know where the money was going to come from. So it happened, that while in prayer, the Lord told me to ask my husband and we sent some money to a pastor and his wife. It was the largest amount of money I had ever given. I had not given this amount to my mother or any of my relatives.

My husband obeyed and we sent the money. When I rang the couple to tell them the good news, they were as amazed as to how quickly God had answered their prayer. They said that the night before they had prayed and God told them that He had already provided and He was going to send the money.

Surprisingly, that was exactly the same word God gave us. He told us that He had already provided and was going to send someone to provide the finance. It seems we were praying at the same time, apart from the time difference.

The same angel who told Mary that she was going to have a Son is the one who told Zacharias about John the Baptist. What a feeling to realise that God can use us as his ears and hands in someone's life. You see, most people want to be used as God's voice but not His ears to hear the voice of those crying, or His hands to help those in need.

Isaiah 59:1
Behold, the Lord's hand is not shortened that it cannot save; nor his ear heavy, that it cannot hear.

The couple had been given days to leave the house they were renting. They also needed money to take their children to school. After doing what God asked us, the following day I received an email from another man I had only met once sometime back in a church where I went to minister.

Initially I had told him about Uganda and my intention to go. I didn't know that God would speak to Him about my trip. In the email he wrote that God had spoken to him to give us some money for Uganda and also to pay for our flights. He didn't stop there. He ended up coming with us all the time we were there. God used him to speak to and bless many people.

As if that was not enough, when we came back God spoke to him to partner with my ministry financially.

God used us as angels in other people's needs because He was also going to send His angel to meet our needs. What a blessing to be used in angelic ministry.

## Begging

Once we know our God and what He is capable of doing, we can't be beggars. The day we accept Jesus into our lives, He frees us from the beautiful gate to a beautiful beginning.

A beautiful gate is a place of disabled and disadvantaged people. These people rely on others to determine their day because they have no choice to do anything.

The Bible talks of a beggar who sat at the entry of the beautiful gate for many years. People who entered the temple gave him coins, which would not deliver him from his situation. The coins he collected were just enough to keep him alive, but he still remained at the gate.

Begging is a curse that only sets you in a position to view others enter their destiny and success, but you can never get there. You watch others pass by and progress while you are stuck in the same position.

When you visit cities in third world countries, you find beggars have positioned themselves in good spots where everyone passing is able to see them. They are carried back to that very position every day.

I talk to people who prefer to beg instead of trusting God for open doors. The people you beg to carry your dream can only give you support to a certain point and then continue to their destinations.

Having discovered the wealth in the word of God, I made a decision never to beg people for just enough for a day, but to trust Him who meets my hearts desires.

Begging suppresses the potential and the ability in you to dance to other people's tunes even when the music is not your liking. You also become a battlefield for the giants who want to use you or step on you to achieve their selfish ambitions.

Luke 16:20-
But there was a certain beggar named Lazarus, full of sores, who was laid at his gate.21 desiring to be fed with the crumbs which fell from the rich man's table.Moreover the dogs came and licked his sores.

Being a beggar puts you in a vulnerable position that when you cry for help, people won't listen to you. They are familiar with your voice and they don't care even when you are in a serious condition. They only wait to hear of the day you die and be taken away from the gate.

For example, whenever the media shows many children in third world countries dying of hunger and malnutrition, it doesn't really raise many concerns. As well as in the developed world, children including unborn babies, are valued and protected by law.

When a baby dies during birth, the issue can make headlines. The authorities will demand to know the cause of that death so that it won't happen again. One unborn baby is heard over the thousands who die every day.

Third world leaders have failed to get their people out of the beautiful gate to walk through it. The begging spirit has bound people's minds that even those who can afford to help, can't help the poor, but they steal what is donated to the poor to make themselves names and so be considered important.

When Peter and John, who had everything the crippled man needed arrived, they said to him, "Gold and silver we don't have but in the name of Jesus rise up and walk". I am quite sure they too had some money but they knew that his problem was not going to be solved financially but this man needed a supernatural healing from God.

They saw that man had a lot of potential but his dreams were dormant as long as he was still sitting at the beautiful gate.

They were not there to give him the surplus that everyone else was giving. Their goal was to get him to walk through the beautiful gate into a place of personal freedom. He was able to walk to the temple for the first time and worship God in truth and Spirit. People who had been ignoring him, raised their heads to see whether he was the one who had been sitting at the beautiful gate. He was uplifted from being a beggar to a celebrity. You see, when celebrities pass they attract a lot of attention. Everyone wants to take photos with them and have their signatures on their various possessions.

God wants to elevate some of you from where you have been, through the beautiful gate, so your dreams will unfold quickly. So many opportunities are going to seek after you.

You can't become a public figure, and fail to get attention from the media. Every TV and radio station would like to broadcast your story. You are going to make headlines in all the news reports because your story is different and so fascinating. Everyone wants to know how it feels to sit at the beautiful gate.

Jesus cannot come into our lives, walk through our communities or nation and we remain the same. Wherever Jesus passes he sets everything as new and beautiful. He shows them what God has always intended them to be.

I want people to get out of the beautiful gate mindset to a beautiful beginning.

Peter came upon the mountains of hopelessness in the man's life with the good news of a beautiful beginning and raised him to the mountain of God.

Isaiah 52:
'How beautiful upon the mountains are the feet of him who brings good news, who proclaims peace, who brings glad tidings of good things, who proclaims salvation, who say to Zion, your God reins.

Matt 21:22
And whatever things you ask in prayer, believing you will receive.

Luke 11:9
So I say to you, ask, and it will be given you, seek, and you will find; knock and it will be opened to you.

John 11:22
But even now I know that whatever you ask of God, God will give you.

When Jesus saw us, we were beggars and poor. He came and gave His priceless life's blood to own us. He made us a royal priesthood. Kings don't beg, they command. The same is true with priests. They don't beg but they ask and stand before God on behalf of others.

We should elevate our minds from wanting to be beggars, to being transformers of lives like Peter and John. The Bible says do to others what you want to be done to you. God is calling the church to give what we have, what is best for us. This is not the second best.

God didn't ask Abraham for Ishmael. He asked him for Isaac, his only son. Abraham had two sons, but why did God ask him for his "only" son? What is more valuable to you can be just as valuable to someone else.

The same happiness and joy you get while in your comfort zone is what someone else would love to have. God wants us to bless someone in the same manner we are called. If you are wealthy God wants you to make someone else wealthier. In fact, when Peter prayed for the man, he gained fame in one day. It took Peter years of trying to advance from being a fisherman to an apostle.

Be not concerned when you see someone you help prosper more than you. The only way to evaluate and realise your value is when those you help succeed and become better than you.

I have heard people say, "So and so was only poor but when I began helping them, they are now possessing all these expensive things". The question is, what was your motive in helping? Did you want to see that person's life changed or did you want to see it to gain praise from people.

A friend of mine told me that one time they were in a family meeting and her rich brother stood up and asked everyone to tell him their problems so that he could help them. She was given a scholarship by a certain organisation, to go and study in the U.K. but she was to pay her own way. The person she thought would help was her brother. She went and told him hoping he would help her. But when he heard about the opportunity, he changed his mind and said he didn't have the money to waste.

In that very week, a relative died and he was quick to respond and pay for all the funeral expenses. He would rather put his money in the dead than helping his sister to go forward.

## If You Don't do it Now Then You Will Never be Able to Help

One day I got a phone call from a man of God in Uganda. It was at 4.00 a.m. Uganda time. He asked me to financially support him because God had spoken to him at the beginning of the year to go to America. He had some money but it was less than he needed. When he told me about it, I told him I was not in position to help for I had many bills to pay.

After he had got off the phone I heard a clear voice speaking to me: "if you don't help him now then you will never be able to do so". I asked myself why is it that he called me at that early hour and never phoned someone else. The voice said to me, "You sow in faith, you reap in faith".

Immediately I went on Facebook and sent him a message that we were going to send him the money he needed. The next day his response was that after he had stopped talking to me, the Lord asked him to go ahead and book his ticket for He had already paid for it. And he was wondering whether it was God who spoke to him or his own voice. He then said that the morning before he woke up to pray, the Lord had told him that I was the one going to give him the money. Even though I wasn't ready to bless him, the Lord had already stirred up my heart to give before I knew of the situation.

I believe God choose me to do this because I had asked Him to use me to change lives. I asked Him to use me to give people beautiful beginnings. I told Him, "God, for me to know that I am blessed by you I want to see you move through the people you use me to help. I may not give them a lump sum, but every seed I sow, whether in someone in business or school fees, I want it to germinate and prosper."

The Bible tells us that every man will give an account of his life before God. I want to be fruitful by helping people to help others.

When the man of God came from America, God had blessed him abundantly. I didn't give him the abundance but God used me as a road to his success. I am so grateful to God that he honoured me by giving me that opportunity, not someone else.

Things like this makes me think and wonder who am I that God loved so much to trust me with part of His kingdom bank where His people enter and make withdrawals? What I mean here is when people ask God for provision and He directs them to me, He provides, though I don't have large resources. It shows me that God has trusted me with His invisible wealth and faith is the debit card I use to make withdrawals from His account. He says, if you will be faithful with little, God will trust you with great things. I was in my home thinking of other things rather than God was thinking of me by sending his servant to bless me.

## The cost of partnering with God

Psalm 126:5-6
Those who sow in tears shall reap in joy. V6 He who continually goes forth weeping, bearing seed for sowing, shall doubtless come again with rejoicing, bringing his sheaves with him.

We read the story of a rich young man who wanted to follow Jesus but when He asked him to go back and sell all his belongings and give to the poor, he found it hard to make that decision even after having kept all the commandments. He thought that by being faithful to all the basic laws he would be worthy to follow Jesus. Jesus assured him that to be His follower, it was not just to keep the law but to walk a sacrificial life.

Jesus wanted him to follow Him with all his life and not leave anything behind to be a reason for him to turn back. Jesus didn't ask him to give everything away but He wanted him to convert his heavy load into Jesus' light one.

In other words, Jesus wanted to own him and his business so that he might live a blessed and successful life and business in Him.

When we follow Christ that means we belong to Him and everything that belongs to us is His. Jesus wants us not only to follow him but to also do business with Him. Jesus himself is a business man and the name of his company is called giving. He gave everything of His to us so that we might also make Him more profits by giving to others.

He advises us to invest our riches in the kingdom of God where there are no robbers, moths or rust. When we do business with Christ, we are not to be affected by the world economy that is designed to steal our peace.

Partnering with God can be painful sometimes. The Bible says, for God so loved the world that He gave his only Son. Abraham, so obeyed God that he offered his only son. Love is equal to obedience.

It was Abraham's obedience that moved God to give us His only Son. The Bible tells us that Jesus is the only Lamb of God Who was offered as a ransom of our sins. There are no more Lambs in heaven.

The substitute lamb that Abraham saw in the bush was a picture of Jesus Himself. God gave us Jesus in the same way Abraham obeyed to give Him Isaac. Just as Isaac was the only son of Abraham so was Jesus the only Son of God.

When we give God our best, He also gives us His best. He who continually goes forth weeping carrying precious seed to sow comes again rejoicing, not he who goes once rejoicing carrying the seed to sow.

To partner with God we have to give things that leave wounds in our hearts so that God himself may heal us in due season. My dear, I want to bring to your attention that if you don't feel any pain in your giving you are missing God's blessings that add no sorrow.

By not feeling pain means you are not giving what costs you something. Probably God would have not have given us Jesus if Abraham gave Ishmael instead of Isaac. I want us to ask ourselves, how many times, have we missed the heavenly blessings that could have changed our lives, our world and future generations for being greedy with the little things that we think we possess. God has promised to send revival and the latter glory but it has to come at a cost.

We have to give everything we think is valuable and adorable to us.

When Abraham stretched out his hand and took the knife to slay his son, the Angel of the Lord called to him from heaven and said, do not lay your hand on the lad or do anything to him; for now "I know that you fear God", since you have not withheld your son, your only son from Me. Then Abraham lifted his eyes and looked and there behind him was a ram. He offered it up for a burnt offering instead of his son.

We have talked and preached sermons on Abraham being the father of faith. Do we think it was easy for him to acquire that honour? By giving his son, it meant that he gave back everything God had blessed him with. He gave back all his long time savings that had taken him years to save and gave all his future hope.

In Uganda we have seasons for sowing and it happens that during these same seasons, this is the time when food is scarce. I remember as a young girl, I used to wonder why my parents wouldn't give us vegetables, corn, beans and nuts they had stored to eat. Rather, they planted them in the ground.

It wasn't until I grew up and learned that if you want more seeds you have to sow some in the ground to grow.

My parents and other farmers made the decision to sacrifice their hunger and sow more food for the future because they had the vision of plenty. Let's not allow situations to limit us from securing our future. What we do today determines what will happen in the future. When I tell people that I know my future, They asked me how do I know?

The answer is because I know that my investments are with God. I don't doubt my future by any situation, for I know business with God doesn't make losses.

Sometimes God can tell you to give things your family maybe in need of.

It was not easy for Abraham to leave his family and go to the place where God would show him. Doing something for your family members doesn't hurt like doing something for a stranger.

Sometimes when your family members learn that you are doing things for other people and not them, they may resent it. Why? You are walking a journey of faith and they are not sure where you are going. They think you are risking your life. That's why they try to show their concern in stopping you from going. It is very hard to pay attention to the things of God when there are other voices telling you reasons why you shouldn't.

The enemy has used ourselves to hinder us from being elevated to the great promises of God. If we limit ourselves by the daily demands in life, we are limiting the greatest harvest that the world has ever seen.

Matt 12:36
And a man's enemies will be those of his own household.V37 He who loves father or mother more than me is not worthy of me. And he who loves son or daughter more than me is not worthy of me.V38 And he who does not take his cross and follow after me is not worthy of me.V39 He who finds his life will lose it, and he who loses his life for my sake will find it.

Isaiah 60:2
For behold, the darkness shall cover the earth and deep darkness the people But the Lord will arise over you, and His glory will be seen upon you.

God is looking for the church that will radiate His glory, a church that will be a lighthouse when the earth is covered in darkness, a church that will open the eyes of the blind, like the crippled man sitting at the entrance of the temple not knowing whether help was on the way or not.

The world is at the point where it is doing everything to save the worsening situation. We have had many temples that have put people at the beautiful gate and consoling them but are not solving the problem.

God is after a church, a body that will fulfil people's needs, and a church that will not just try but will do great exploits. People are tired of words they want to see the works of the Holy Spirit.

## Revival is in you

The revival the world is waiting for is in you. You could be delaying it because you are not sensitive to the particular season. If a woman doesn't know the time she conceives, she cannot know the due time for her delivery unless she goes for a scan.

The scanner for revival is earnest prayer. You need to labour before God until you get exhausted, pray until you get lost for words when speaking to Him in His presence. I want to tell you that at the last minute when a woman feels like "I can't do this anymore", is the very time she gains the strength to bring the baby to birth.

The effort of that last attempt is gained through her decision to get that baby born.Pray to steer and position that revival in the birth canal because it may die if it's overdue.

Whenever revival is to be birthed, two signs appear. A sign that appears in heaven to give birth and a sign that appears in heaven to devour or hinder that birth.

People claim to be waiting for revival but at the same time they are the very people seeking to destroy it. When a person or church starts labouring to give birth to a good cause, it is this very same time the opposition starts labouring an alternative, negative reason against the good one.

One womb carries the baby but many people are involved in its arrival. The doctors, nurses, relatives and friends are all concerned that the safety of the baby be paramount. As soon as the baby is born, every participant's goal is achieved.

Ask yourself, if you are not a sign of distraction, then who are you? Are you a mother, a doctor, a nurse or a relative? Whoever person you maybe, you are important in the birth of revival.

It's impossible to see a doctor or nurse telling a woman to vacate the birthing bed so that another person may replace the woman to give birth to the baby. The disorder and the negligence that has been going on in the birthing suit has made the revival overdue.

A birthing suit is a place of a purpose. Every participant knows what their roles are immediately they walk through the door. Everyone, including a young child, knows what takes place in a birthing suit.

The way we conduct ourselves in churches doesn't bring revival. Everyone wants to be what they feel like being instead of what God wants them to be. God is calling us to get back to His purpose.

He is in the business of introducing new things, new revelations, and new moves.

The challenge we have in churches is we are so used to the move of God causing knew things to happen. Everyone has his or her own doctrine that is opposed to the purpose of God. The people who killed Jesus are those who taught about His coming and were even prepared for his coming based on their earthly understanding.

In order to see the revival proceeding from us, we have to die to our own understandings first and then allow God to do things His way, the way He wants.

Men have spent years studying on revival but why is it not happening? The trouble is, when what we have been waiting for arrives we don't receive it. For example, when the church asks God to bring healing or transformation and God raises up one member for that purpose or even send someone from somewhere else, the way we are familiar with doing things can lead to missing God's move.

So once those people don't get accepted, they go and start their own "move". This is where we see many churches breaking apart and starting all the time.

Thank God that despite the opposition Mary and Joseph went through with baby Jesus, they didn't run away from the temple and the people God had purposed Jesus for.

They went into exile to escape the threat of death to their child but they brought him back to the place of His purpose. It's alright to run for the safety of your dream but don't migrate. The promise is a promise and it is fulfilled in the place where it is designed to be.

If we endure and remain patient, positioned in the right places, one day there will be men like Simeon. They may be blind but spiritually alert to bless your dream inside the temple.

Running away with a non-blessed dream can land you in trouble. Revival allows the Holy Spirit to shape our characters in line with the word and the will of God. Until we get to that point where our communities sense and feel this godly character in us, we are not any different from others.

We will know that revival is at hand when we see the world calling us derogatory names and mocking the godly character that is hidden inside us. When the revival is in us, we don't introduce it but it introduces us wherever we go.

Early church people were named Christians by people who saw Jesus working through the church. The church didn't go around telling people that they were Christians. The character of Jesus in them drove them to do extraordinary things that captured people's attention.

A true Christian cannot hide, something in you will cause people around you, even those you don't know, to ask if you are a Christian.

Acts 4:32
Now the multitude of those who believed were of one heart and one soul; neither did anyone say that any of the things he possessed was his own, but they had all things in common.

They were sharing everything together without anyone claiming that their possessions were theirs.

As we continue to read, somewhere I will share about what sharing the anointing can cause. Why was it necessary for the church to share everything?

It was not until I came to Australia that I understood the concept of sharing everything. In Australia when families, churches or groups come together, everyone brings a plate, (they call it BYO), bring your own. By doing this it doesn't put pressure on one person to prepare meals. It also allows them to taste different varieties brought by different people. It also saves time for the host, creating enough time to socialise with others.

We are all broken pieces of revival that need the broken pieces put together. When we share, it simplifies the work of God. What we have, another church doesn't have and what every church has, we all need it. We all need one another in order to be a complete and glorious church of our Lord Jesus.

# CHAPTER FIVE

# REPENTANCE

2 Peter 3
The Lord is not slack concerning his promise, as some count slackness, but is longsuffering toward us, not willing that any should perish but that all should come to repentance.

I shared about how the whole community of Budadiri East was disgusted with the behaviour of the churches and their pastors. They worked so hard and were always busy in their ministries but there was no impact on the community.

Once God purposes to work in a place or in someone and the people continue to do what they think they can in their own strength, He waits until that person fails, then God enters the situation. Man's extremity is God's opportunity.

God had a great plan for the community but He was waiting for the church to come into alignment with His word before He started to show Himself.

The time came when every church became desperate to witness the move of God and as they continued to pray and seek the face of God, He said, "Repent and turn back to me with all your hearts".

This makes us wonder, were not these churches exercising repentance? Definitely they did. I remember sometimes we would be in the middle of worship and then the prophet would stand up and say that God wants us to repent of our sins. The whole church would get on their knees and start to repent and cry. Some people would lay flat on the altar and cry aloud while confessing their sins. But why did God kept on wanting people to repent and turn back to Him?

Repentance is not just confession of our sins, it's about our perception and perspective towards the things of God. It's turning away from what we think we know, to the lordship of the Holy Spirit.

People have had great promises but nothing was happening, why? Because they were not willing to walk the path with the Holy Spirit who knew where the promises were. Sometimes we think that it will be because of our much effort that will in turn move God to work. God simply wants us to be obedient to his Spirit.

Have you ever been in a position where you planned something for a very long time, and after putting in all the effort, the Holy Spirit says it's not what He wants from you? You cannot see the reason but after you obey, the promised harvest takes place.

There is a true story of a man of God whom God told to build Him a house. According to his understanding he thought that God had asked him to build a physical building church since the one he was in was falling apart.

The mistake he made was, he did not ask God for clarification but he just assumed to know what God meant. He went in his own strength and encouraged the church members to give and they began laying the foundation.

As they were about to finish, the Lord spoke to the pastor that the house he had built was not a perfect one and therefore asked him to start building again.

The pastor took some time to ask God what He meant. The Lord told him that He wanted him to build with souls, not a physical house. As the pastor obeyed and told the members, some people got offended and left the church wondering whether the pastor had had problems with his mind.

When he decided to go around churches bringing the message of repentance, many people understood the meaning of true repentance and turned back to God. Some of them had been in churches for a very long time without changing including the leaders. As he continued to build souls, the Lord blessed him mightily and asked him to begin building churches for different ministries. Now if this man had looked at himself and considered what people said, he would have not achieved all those blessings.

King David wanted to build a house for God to express his gratitude. But God, who searches the hearts saw that David's hands were full of bloodshed and he needed to cleanse himself. He was unworthy to build God a house.

God is not after the great things we do for Him but he wants our hearts to turn back to him in such a way He may work through us. He says His eyes are moving to and fro in the whole earth looking for the man whose heart is perfect before Him that He may strongly support him. How many times we struggle with the things of God and are always asking Him for support? If our hearts are perfect before God, we are not required to ask Him for support because His support will be automatic.

After the pastors realised that God wanted their hearts more than what they were striving for, they began asking God in which way He wanted them to turn back to Him.

God began speaking to them about the unity of his body. He said as long as there was still division, He was not going to elevate any church, irrespective of how much they prayed and fasted.

God knew that if He lifted one church above others, there would be a lot of jealousy, hatred and strife. He doesn't build His church on competition but on humility. He therefore asked the church to humble themselves in unity that He himself would build Himself a glorious church that would display His glory. He wanted to build Himself a church without walls in the community.

Psalm 122:1
Unless the Lord builds the house, they labour in vain who build it. Unless the Lord guards the city, the watchman stays awake in vain.

## Plumbline

A plumbline is a line from which a weight is suspended to determine verticality or depth.

Plumblines are used for measuring the perfection of building walls. No builder can build without using a plumbline. We see in many scriptures God compares his word as a plumbline.

We saw the word of God declaring not to despise the day of small things as long as the plumbline is in the hand of Zerubbabel, the seven will rejoice.

Zerubbabel was a governor of Judah and being a governor, he was in the position to make good or bad choices for the people of Judah. Many times God would punish innocent people for the sin of their leaders.

Whenever David sinned against God, He would strike the whole nation of Israel with famine and disease. That's why I wrote somewhere about who is leading you.

Apart from preaching, does your leader's life and testimony reflect the word of God? Is he/her holding the plumbline in his hand or compromising the truth.

When you hold the plumbline in your hand, you may be called weird names and not be understood because you stand for the truth that is in you.

When I came to Australia I was told many times that the word I should speak to Australians should be different from Africans. At first I developed fear and inadequacy speaking to Australians. I thought that every time I spoke I would be speaking a Ugandan message that would offend people.

Thank God, that though I was told this, I didn't compromise my plumbline. I went back to God and asked him if He knew that I only knew a Ugandan message, why did he bring me to Australia?

There is nowhere in the Bible where God has given us different Scriptures for different places or people. However, if God sends us to different places, He has given the grace and Holy Spirit that we should rely on to show us what we should say to His people.

You see, as we continue taking the nations for Christ, we will be confronted by strongholds and people trying to pull us back to their level where they have previously blocked others. You will find those advising you on how things are done according to them. I am not saying that they are wrong but still you have to follow God's Spirit. He knows whether what they do is wrong or not.

If you are a missionary or an apostle, you have to know whenever God sends you to a place, He wants you to take down some things and rebuild. You can't do this great work without a plumbline in your hand. You are a great builder sent to rebuild the broken and collapsing walls.

Jeremiah 1:9-10

Then the Lord put forth His hand and touched my mouth, and the Lord said to me: Behold I have put my words in your mouth. See I have this day set you over the nations and over the kingdoms to root out and to pull down, to destroy and to throw down, to build and to plant.

## Seven

Revelation 1:4
John, to the seven churches which are in Asia and who was and who is to come, and from the seven spirits who are before his throne.

The seven rejoice to see the plumbline in the hand of Zerubbabel. Seven is a symbolic qualitative number conveying the idea of completeness and when related to God, the idea of perfection. The seven who rejoice are the seven Spirits who are before the throne of God. The seven Spirits picture the Holy Spirit in His manifold and perfect dynamic activity. The seven "lamps of fire" suggest His illuminating, purifying and energizing ministries. The seven Spirits are before the throne and simultaneously speak the seven eyes of the lamb.

Revelation 4:5
And from the throne proceeded lightning's, thundering and voices. Seven lamps of fire were burning before the throne which are the seven Spirits of God.

The Holy Spirit is ready to move in his fullness. He is waiting to see his chosen ones govern the world apart from the hands of evil powers. He is not worried about how small it starts but as soon as the plumbline is in their hands, the revival is going to spread like fire.

Haggai 1:1

The first people that the word of God came to through prophet Haggai was Zerubbabel and Joshua. Zerubbabel was a governor and Joshua was a priest. Zerubbabel represents the government or the kingdom and Joshua represents the church or the body of Christ today. If God is going to do a new thing in the nation,

There are two strategic positions the Holy Spirit will influence first in reaching His people. These are the church and the government. There is no way we are going to see the move of God in our cities and communities if our government leaders don't acknowledge God's son, Jesus.

It is therefore Joshua's (church) responsibility to stand in the gap and intercede on behalf of our government (Zerubbabel) to pick up the plumbline. We are to earnestly pray and command God to replace top offices with God fearing people, that they may lead our nations in the ways of God.

The Bible says blessed is the nation whose God is the Lord, not the church whose God is the Lord. God is already a father of the church but He wants to be king of our nations through our leaders. That's why when He sent Haggai, He didn't send him to Joshua alone but actually spoke to Zerubbabel first. He wanted both Zerubbabel and Joshua to ascend the mountain with all the people and bring wood to rebuild his temple.

If our governments will become involved in what God is intending to do, not for political reasons but for God's glory, we will see the Spirit sweeping through our land. The seven will rejoice to see the plumbline in Zerubbabel's hand because that will give them an opening to freely flow in enacting the will of God.

Haggai 1:1In the second year of King Darius in the sixth month, on the first day of the month, the word of the Lord came by Haggai the prophet to Zerubabbel the son of Sheltie governor of Judah and to Joshua the son of Jehozadak the high priest, saying:

# CHAPTER SIX

# LORD, "WE" COME TO YOU, NOT, "I "COME TO YOU

2 Chronicles 7:14 If my people who are called by my name will humble themselves and pray and seek my face and turn from their wicked ways, then I will hear from heaven and will forgive their sin and heal their land.

As the pastors gradually began responding to the will of God, they began praying together. During their prayers, they didn't come to God as individuals representing their needs but as a body surrendering to God to do whatever He wanted.

They laid aside all their differences and began afresh in God's will. In these joint prayers, one of the things I realised they didn't do every time was when they appeared before Him, they didn't have prayer requests as they had been doing in their doing in churches. In their churches they made a lot of demands on God. They were praying according to their own fleshly desires. For example, having the biggest church with powerful music. God said, "Your prayers are not answered because you pray with wrong motives".

In these joint prayers they poured out their hearts to God. By doing this, the Holy Spirit began leading them in what to pray for. The main area the Holy Spirit led the pastors to pray without ceasing was to cry for lost souls. It was during this moment that this was the only time I have felt the Spirit of God groaning in people's hearts for lost souls. It was during this moment that I realised that as much as we are asking God to build churches and other worthwhile pursuits, that what really matters to Him is lost souls. Before, we were finding ways of fulfilling our dreams, yet God was saying if you only turn your hearts to Me I will show you My heart's desire. Jesus didn't die for us in order to have these all these peripheral things but He died for the lost. If we will continue to intercede for the lost, then all these things will be freely given to us without cost.

As they continued to seek God, He began giving them strategies of soul winning. I said before, that sometimes people refuse to turn to Christ because they don't see any difference in those who claim to follow the Master.

When you see people who haven't given their lives to Christ in your families, communities, villages or cities, before you rush to judge them, first examine your own relationship with God. Woe unto those obstructing God's people from coming in for they will be first to be judged. Woe to those who become stumbling blocks to children and the unsaved. It is better for them that a millstone be hung around their necks and they be cast into the sea.

God has wanted to save the lost but there was no way it was going happen if the church was still hard-hearted. But as soon as the church aligned her heart to the will of God, He began using the pastors to reach His people. God poured a hunger and thirst for his word where everywhere a crusade was staged, people came to Christ running. People began having dreams when the pastors were telling them to give their lives to Christ.

As leaders and Christians in general, whenever we align ourselves to God's righteousness, God uses our images in His appearances or visitations to His people. Remember, God created us in His image so when He uses His appearances to us, that means He is fulfilling His purpose for our existence.

Before, there was a lot of crime almost every day. Every year at least four or five people would be burned to death due to mob justice. The police had become powerless to stop them.

During seasons like Christmas, families would be worried by thugs robbing them in the night. Around that season there would be a lot of evil going on generally but when God began moving all that stopped. It's only God who can guard the city through his righteous people. He says righteousness exalts a nation but evil brings it to disgrace.

God elevated His church to the extent that every Christmas, the non-believers, including Muslims, would demand a crusade for the word of God to be preached. These were the people who incurred all the costs to facilitate the meetings until they concluded.

The people who didn't know Jesus learned how to tap into the blessings of God. When God's presence came down, giving was instant. We didn't have to struggle explaining to people the importance of giving. Once people become hard-hearted to the word of God you can identify them through the lack in their giving.

I see very many leaders struggling with people for them to give towards God's work. I want you to know that if God called you and gave you a task to fulfil, you don't have to struggle with people to make your heart right with God. He will fulfil it.

We saw that as soon as David humbled himself before God, God told him that his son Solomon would be the one to build Him a house. God honoured David's request through his son. The son built a house that made God pleased and promised to establish it and His name forever.

2 Chronicles 7:15-16
Now my eyes will be open and my ears attentive to prayer made in this place. For now I have chosen and sanctified this house that my name may be there forever and my eyes and my heart will be there perpetually.

In these joint meetings God began knitting the hearts of Christians in love for one another and all differences were taken away. They began working together by supporting one another irrespective of which church they attended. Every time they organised conferences or prayer meetings in any church or county, they witnessed the glory of God because everyone got involved.

The move of God didn't stop at gatherings, or even churches on Sundays. New converts gave their lives to Christ all the time and churches began to expand very rapidly.

That kind of oneness caused the Holy Spirit to move and speak to all churches identically. Whenever the pastors came together after church for a meal, they wondered how God influenced them speak the same message. Getting the same messages gave them the clear direction where God was taking them and what He wanted them to do for the community.

Christians who used to run around churches looking for words to spread rumours, stopped and settled because they knew whatever they would say against any church or pastor, they would now be accountable for it.

## Sharing the Anointing

1 Samuel 1: Then Jonathan and David made a covenant because he loved him as his own soul. And Jonathan took off the robe that was on him and gave it to David, with his armour, even to his sword and his bow and his belt.

These are very significant items that Jonathan gave David. First of all, the robe represents covering and protection. Armour also represents strong covering or protection. The sword represents war, aggression, power. A bow is a weapon together with arrows gives the capability to shoot at enemies. The belt represents truth.

In Ephesians 6: 10-18 we see Paul warning the church of Christ to put on the whole armour of God that we may be able to withstand in evil days.

For Jonathan to give David all his military gear and not remain with any, shows he was submitting under David's authority and kingship. He was also passing on all his rights of being a future king of the throne of Israel, to David. He did that after sensing that the favour and grace of God upon him to rule people was gone. Jonathan didn't try to persecute or fight David because they were in a blood covenant relationship and were best friends. The Bible questions us, how can two walk together unless they agreed.

Covenant relationship means whatever is yours belongs to me. God had passed judgment upon the house of Saul, Jonathan's father, from being king together with his blood line for disobedience. But when the time came that the whole of Saul's bloodline had been killed except Jonathan's crippled son, David then remembered his covenant with Jonathan and spared him by letting his son live. Not only that, but he also organised a big feast and commanded his son to be brought and seated next to him.

The power of a covenant is even if someone is dead, his blood will remain alive. By David bringing the crippled son to his table, he was honouring Jonathan to let him know that they were both kings of Israel.

Jonathan was a king by blood and David was a king in the natural realm. David knew that if he killed Jonathan's son, he would have destroyed himself and his kingdom.

The Bible says Jesus is the King of Kings and subsequently has made us kings through His blood that lives in us. He is not here to fight for us but His blood in us gives us victory against all our adversaries. He wants His blood to rule the earth through us.

We may ask ourselves how unwise Jonathan was to pass his kingdom to a stranger without even a fight. Has God ever asked you to do things that seem like they are contrary to your favour? Responding obediently to such circumstances is where the hidden blessings of God are.

I have learned one thing in my life: to obey God in everything He tells me knowing that no instruction of His is going to be against me.

After Jonathan sensed that the kingdom had been passed into other hands, he knew that the only way to retain leadership was to make a covenant with David, and consequently passed the mantle to David.

When God decides to change something, the best way we benefit is to ask Him for wisdom as to how we can participate, rather than fighting to hang on to our ways. Once we hang on to things, we find ourselves being used by the enemy to destroy what we struggled for.

Many years ago, God used western missionaries to bring the gospel to Africa. When they came, they said God was going to use Africans to bring revival and the gospel of righteousness to the west. They found Africa was very fertile ground in which to sow the word of God.

Africans treasured the word and began to fast and seek God, They spent weeks and months on Prayer Mountains to see the word spoken to them come to pass. God heard their prayers and began sending them to the western nations.

But the disappointing thing was, some western leaders and pastors failed to reap the fruit their ancestors laboured for. They were not willing to sit and enjoy the harvest but became stubborn and hard-hearted.

God has sent so many African missionaries to the west but the westerners are not ready to honour God through Africans. They probably look at them and think what good can come out of Africa, the people we help? A rich man, whenever he sees someone who is not of his level of society knocking at their gate, he thinks they have come to beg. The rich mindset has corrupted western leaders into thinking that every African missionary they see is there to promote their orphanages back home. The devil has blinded the western church from embracing God's visitation through their poor judgment.

Once Africans see that they are not received in churches, they also end up opening their own African churches. I wonder if truly in heaven there will be African, Chinese or Samoan churches. What if a non-Samoan goes to a Samoan church, will he be received and will he not offend the Samoan spirit?

The Bible says all nations will come together in worshiping God and His Son Jesus in one language saying "Hallelujah". The way we integrate here on earth trains us as to how we will be in heaven. Hallelujah is the language everyone should be practising, otherwise many will be shocked when we get to heaven and realise that all other languages don't exist.

When I had just arrived in Australia, a pastor called my husband and I for a meeting. He said to me that he wanted me to pastor an African church. I said to myself Lord have mercy upon your people for the racist attitude. If you knew that you called me only for Africans, then why did you take me from Africa to Australia?

The pastors of Budadiri East came to realise that if their ministries were of God, then the people they lead belong to Him. Therefore, the purpose of their repentance was to be each his brother's keeper. Christ died on the cross to establish a new covenant that binds everyone together as one. When they betray each other's churches or ministries, they would, in fact, be destroying their own. They formed a slogan which declares, "Fellow fighters, help me to help you fulfil our visions and callings from God. Divided we fall. United we stand as an army of God."

They knew that God had called them to faithfully pastor His flock through trembling and fear. He had called each with a different grace yet they needed each other in their churches. So when they started exchanging churches each Sunday, they exposed all the five-fold ministries to their people.

Previously, if the pastor had a teaching ministry, his church would produce teachers only. If a pastor was an evangelist he would develop evangelists. They learned that such minor differences were basically the cause of the differences they had. They also noticed that as much as they were inviting visiting preachers to their churches, if they didn't take full responsibility for each other's churches, Christians would not now believe in them.

This helped them in a huge area so that when any one of them travelled away, the church of Christ continued functioning and multiplied normally. Christians then, didn't look to one pastor, but they would go to any pastor available.

Through unity, they have been able to detect any false religion that tries to come into the community. The government has given them the right to examine everyone who starts a Church. The first thing they do is to examine doctrine to see whether it's of God. Only then they support that person to become established.

When the time came for me to move to Australia, people became concerned as to who I was going to leave in authority in the church. Even when I reached Australia, every person I told that I was pastoring a church in Uganda showed the same concern: "Whom did you leave your church with? Are Christians going to other churches?"

Working together with other men and women of God lifted the load that would have concerned me. Probably I would be settled in one place thinking that when I left the church would collapse. I have been in Australia for many years, yet the men and women of God continue to look after the church like their own. They have managed to raise ministers as usual. You really need to be there to understand what God is doing.

We work together so that even when I am far away and ask them to mobilize conferences or do anything for me in the church, they successfully put everything together.

Oh how interesting ministry can be when we learn to trust and work together? Jesus promised us to learn from him for His burden or yoke is light. He knew that when we work together, ministry will be interesting.

I told God that if He helps me to write this book, all the proceeds will be sown into these pastors for the great work God is using them to do. It is one of the ways I can contribute to these lovely servants of God.

My heart's desire is to see them living a good and adorable lifestyle that is worthy of their labour and toil in the kingdom. God has used them and is still using them to do amazing work amidst tough challenges they face as I will share with you later. I want them to have decent homes as they continue to do the great work of our Lord Jesus Christ.

## Sharing Burdens

So Jesus said to them "because of your unbelief, for assuredly, I say to you, if you have faith as a mustard seed, you will say to this mountain: move from here to there, and it will move and nothing will be impossible for you."

Faith without works is dead. Yet if we have as little faith as a mustard seed, the mountains would move.

Basically, the main cause of having many orphans and single mothers in Uganda or Africa at large, is irresponsible men eloping with young girls and having children to them. They then dump them and continue looking for more young girls.

As these men continue changing women all the time, they end up acquiring HIV aids which some of them bring back to the first girls, now so-called wives and pass the disease on to them. One man might have five to ten women and every woman might have 1 to 10 children and some children are not even known to him.

The pastors saw this as a big generational problem that might never be stopped. However, much the developed world can help. The assistance does not reduce the problem but instead it encourages men to continue being irresponsible, knowing that there are people out there who will help the children.

When we try to fix a problem without knowing the cause and how to prevent it, it gets worse. They realised that it was their responsibility and so they then identified ways of solving the problem gradually.

Among the new converts that God brought to churches, were youth. The youth were so passionate in seeking and serving the Lord. The pastors continuously encouraged them never to be involved in sexual acts until they got married to one partner. They also watched over them and encouraged them to pray and trust God to guide them in choosing their marriage partners.

Finally, as the youth walked their journey of faith in having happy marriages, they were faced with huge mountains that some couldn't afford to move unless they were supported by other members of the Body. It was the mountain of dowries from the girl's families.

Some families ask a lot of money or cows and other gifts based on their daughters' education.

Because they didn't want the youth they laboured so much in disappointing them by eloping with girls. The pastors stood together by raising money and other things needed to pay dowries for those who could not afford to.

Giving someone a cow or a goat is a big thing in Uganda. The person has to be either a close relative or very important to someone. But the love and the unity of God moves the precious believers to give and do other important things for the brides who they are not related to.

This burden would have been very hard for one church but because all the churches got involved, the contributions are realised in one day. The spirit of unity and love of God stirs people's hearts to give cheerfully. Giving is not a burden but a blessing to them. They love giving without expecting anything in return because they know that God is a giver who in turn loves cheerful givers. They don't have much to give but everyone rushes to give the little he or she has.

## Why a Dowry is paid

I am sure most of you, once you read about a dowry, you are asking this very question "why is a dowry paid?" I am writing to clarify it. I myself used to oppose it because of the way the girl's family would treat the boy's family if their demands were not met. Sometimes, it gets so impossible for the boy's family until ultimately his family decides not to give their child's hand in marriage. This puts such a lot of pressure and disappointment on a girl resulting in some of them taking their lives or running away with the boy to never to be seen again.

A dowry is a good thing and it is Biblical when it is done in free will or just gifts that have no harsh conditions. But some poor minded and inconsiderate families make it extremely difficult because of their ridiculous demands.

Basically, a dowry is meant to be full of fun in bringing two parties or families together to know each other and then become one family for the sake of their children getting married.

It also helps to identify those who will be responsible in the event their children going through marriage challenges. These people provide them with counselling and marital knowledge before they get married.

The dowry is based on Genesis 24. How Abraham sent his servant to go and find a wife for his son

Isaac and after finding her the servant gave precious gifts to Rebecca's family.

v53. Then the servant brought out jewellery and silver, jewellery of gold and clothing and gave them to Rebecca. He also gave precious things to her brother and to her mother.

Giving a dowry is like a blessing from the boy's family to the girl's family appreciating and honouring them for allowing their son to marry their daughter. It also shows the girl's parents how precious their daughter is, that every precious thing is worth working for as it is very costly.

The Bible says that when Jacob looked at Rachael and thought she was beautiful, he worked for fourteen years to have her. At the end of the first seven years he was given the wrong woman but this did not stop him from getting what he wanted. He worked a further seven years and got what he wanted.

The marriages that last in Africa are the ones where men have paid a dowry for their wives. If a woman lives with a man who doesn't want to meet her family, he doesn't think of paying her dowry even if he is rich. You know that, that man doesn't value her and that at any time she might run away. He gets another woman. They know if their men love them by going to meet their families, they bring honour to the woman.

Giving a dowry is like labouring for a precious thing, just as Jacob worked for Rachael.

Sometimes we find ourselves criticising things that we have no clue on their importance and how they work. After coming to know why a dowry exists, I now support it in our African culture, more especially that now God is involved.

It is more glorious to see families and friends gathered celebrating the giveaway which is called the "introduction ceremony". I love it when I see a young boy wanting to marry. I ask my husband and we sow a seed in that marriage.

## Building Churches

Haggai 1:14
So the Lord stirred up the spirit of Zerubbabel the son of Shealtriel, governor of Judah, and the spirit of Joshua, the son of Jehozadak, the high Priest and the spirit of all the remnant of the people and they came and worked on the house of the Lord of hosts, their God.

It is such an amazing experience to see how God has used his servants to rebuild His work. I thank God that He honoured me and called me to be one of a team.

It used to take one church a year to save money to buy one iron sheet for the roofing of the church. The only church you could see roofed with 20 to 50 iron sheets was the one that was affiliated with the western world ministry. What the western ministries do is when the missionaries come, they buy iron sheets and then leave the rest of the work for the local members, in some cases. Then the locals would try hard to raise the shelter and roof it. From then on they would continue having services in an unfinished shelter. Erecting more timber to finish the walls was a struggle, you would see a church in an unfinished state for years.

As for the rest of the churches that didn't have any help from anywhere else, they either used to fellowship under trees or in grass thatched huts. Social bars and witch doctors' shrines looked much better than churches. It was very hard for people to get out of bars to come to such churches.

Haggai 1:5 & 7.We see the Lord telling his people to consider their ways.

# CHAPTER SEVEN

# THE LATTER GLORY OF THE LATTER HOUSE

Haggai 2:4
Yet now be strong Zerubbabel, says the Lord, and be strong Joshua, son of Jehozadak, the high priest; and be strong, all you people of the Lord; says the Lord, and work; for I am with you says the Lord of hosts.

We see many times in the Bible, whenever God wanted to come down to meet the children of Israel, He would ask them to get ready for His arrival by purifying themselves. God's will is that our hearts be moulded into His heart and that we represent His kingdom accordingly by becoming fellow creators on earth. He called David a man after his heart because he was ever repentant.

Repentance is the building material for the inner house. Every time we repent, our inner house gets upgraded to a later model in order that we can sustain the latter glory. Most times we demand God to do new things for us even when we are not ready to renew ourselves in Him.

David's genuine repentance caused God to bless him greatly and manifest his wisdom, power, favour and glory through his son Solomon. Solomon was able to soar high because of the foundation his father laid for him.

The visions God gives us are like our sons. We cannot see God's blessings in them unless we first lay good foundations or beautiful beginnings for them.

Many people forget to play their part and hope to gain the reality of their dreams. They don't know that it is the dream to gain out of their faithfulness with God first of all.

The first words the angel said to Mary, before he even told her the news of her baby boy was, "Rejoice, highly favoured one, the Lord is with you; blessed are you among women".

God wants someone to tell you what you mean to Him, before telling you what He wants you to do? The angel first delivered Mary's status with God before telling her the message from God. He must have been mesmerised. He must have swelled with pride in being the one to carry the message of the coming baby. It was like giving someone to carry something that he was in need of.

For God to favour Mary over all other women on earth to be His Son's mother, He first knew that she would raise Him in God's fear and righteousness because God had seen righteousness in her.

Psalm5:12
For you O LORD, will bless the righteous;
With favour you will surround him as with a shield.

Luke 1:31-32
And behold, you will conceive in your womb and bring forth a son, and shall call His name Jesus. He will be great and will be called the son of the Highest and the Lord God will give Him the throne of his father David.

Revelation 12:5
She bore a male child who was to rule all nations with a rod of iron. And her child was caught up to God and his throne.

When Mary conceived Jesus, so many baby boys were being born but not all women heard from an angel. That's why, when Herod commanded all boys to be killed, the same angel warned Mary and led her to the place of refuge.

When you see ministries collapse, sometimes we are not to pray for them because every son born of God will die but will be resurrected in righteousness and victory. Death is the only way to test whether something was conceived by God or not.

One time we were with other intercessors praying. A lady brought a prayer request to pray for a pastor who was planning to sell his church building and the land to the Muslims. As we all started praying, the Spirit of God told me to tell the others to stop praying for that. He told me to tell them to pray for what was coming in and going out.

At first I couldn't understand why God would let Muslims possess a church premises. I guess even others felt the same.

But when I went back home, the Lord spoke to me that what that man was doing is who he is inside. His heart treasures money more than Me. I didn't ask him to start that church but he started it for his own gains. That's why it's not gaining him anything. He would rather see Christians scattered and sell the church.

The foundation on which we conceive our dreams matters. In the past, the church has focused so much on teaching people about other things like: anointing, leadership, giving etc. They have forgotten to raise and teach people about righteousness and how to maintain the righteousness of God.

Because of that background many strive to start something to prove to themselves and to the public that they are anointed. More damage has been done to the church of Christ than good. People have preached the word of God by words not by works.

## Command Your Son to Work

When we obey God we won't struggle to build our visions, but our visions will build and speak for us because they originated from God. Are you out there working hard to build your vision? Consider your ways first and turn back to God. He didn't give you his Son to become a weight on your shoulders but to lift your burdens from them.

In John 2:2. When everyone was confused and the situation was hopeless, the master of ceremonies was lost for words after being told that the wine was exhausted. It happened during the middle hour of the day when the wedding was getting more exciting for everyone. The bride was about to cut the cake to serve the guests. The master of ceremonies was cheering loud, promising that everyone would eat enough food and drink. I am saying this because I imagine it was the same way African weddings happen.

Then when one of the service men whispered to the MC that the wine had run out. Guess what? There was silence in place for some minutes. The MC went cold as cold as a freezer. Once the master of ceremonies surprisingly goes quiet, everyone gets curious to know what's going on. When they don't understand, they turn heads to one another to exaggerate the situation.

In my own experience, my wedding had gathered people from all corners of Uganda and Kenya. They were expecting the best of everything due to the high class Hotel I had hired. When the master of ceremonies declared there was no food, I saw people turning to their neighbours and some walked away disappointed.

Once something like this happens, the master of ceremonies walks to the bridal party to request them to walk away so that he, himself, can endure the shame and humiliation instead of the bride. The master of ceremonies plays a very big part in a wedding. He carries the whole wedding on his shoulders. He is the mediator between the bride and the invited guests. He has the choice to either make the wedding great or disappointing. But this time the problem appeared in the food department.

Our pastors and leaders have preached to us about promises; they have prophesied great things in our lives, cities and nations. We have waited and waited until we have lost our love of going to church. We have lost faith in God due to what has happened to us. Maybe your marriage has failed and your children have been taken away. You have given so much and nothing has happened up till now. Every job you apply for is rejected.

We are no longer doing God's business with passionate hearts like we once did. Our pastors are dragging us into churches. They are no longer preaching powerful messages because when they spoke nothing happened.

The good news is amidst this hopeless situation.

There was a woman who had come with her Son. No one knew that the Son was a Saviour except the woman herself. She had kept the secret of God for such time like this.

When God sent his angel to tell her that she was going to give birth to a Saviour, no one knew. When she faced all the humiliation and morning sickness during pregnancy, no one knew.

I want to remind you that no one knows your son better than you. There may be some experts who have spent time studying about him, but they can only assume, they cannot dictate what you know about him.

You and your son shared the same DNA and umbilical cord. You are bound together in flesh and blood so that nothing can ever separate you. You have the choice to believe the experts or what God has told you about your son. You have the power to believe the lies of the devil or your dream.

When you gave birth to him in the corral in the middle of a most disgusting smell, no one was there. When the angels came from the east to worship him everyone was sleeping. And finally, when you walked through the desert to save him from the hands of Herod no one fought for you. You went through everything with Joseph, your husband, who in this illustration represents God.

The woman, having known the potential in her Son, couldn't keep quiet or waste her time talking hopeless words. She knew that the time had come for her Son to do something.

You see, people who have visions don't complain when they see things go wrong, they use that opportunity to display the greatness of their dreams.

The lady commanded her Son to do something even though the Son tried to excuse himself by saying that his time had not yet come. She insisted until the son obeyed and performed the miracle of the new wine. Your son hears your voice even though he feels like he still needs to do other things. Keep commanding him through prayer.

God is looking for men and women who will put their sons to work in public places, governments, or places where things can get worse. He says, "Don't be a problem promoter but be a solution".

I pity Christians who whine about what their bosses or governments don't do. Come on woman, rise up and take a stand. God has given you a son to command who brings life wherever he goes. He is telling you in His word that "concerning my father's work, command me." John says, whoever has the Son has life. Your dream is everything, dear.

Isaiah 9:6
For unto us a child is born, unto us a son is given; and the government will be upon his shoulder. And his name will be called, counsellor, mighty God, Everlasting Father, prince of peace.

## A Woman Fights for Her Son to Have a Second Chance at Life

2Kings 4:27
Now when she came to the man of God at the hill, she caught him by the feet, but Gehazi came near to push her away. But the man of God said, "Let her alone; for her soul is in deep distress, and the Lord has hidden it from me, and has not told me."

Every mother can imagine how devastated this woman would have felt. A son means everything to a mother. When the son cries, she cries. When he is happy, she is happy. You can never do anything to a woman's son and think you are harming him alone. Be well assured that you are affecting the mother more.

There are so many stories in the Bible that talk about a woman and her son. There is a unique and instinct bond between a son and his mother that cannot be easily separated, except by death.

However, as much as death was unconquerable, the love for her son made a Shunammite woman forsake everything and run to find a prophet who could raise her son back to life. She came against resistance when she met him, but the power of love directed her to face death until she overcame it. She wasn't willing to see death corrupt her love or bring devastation.

There were many things that happened in the past that caused the church forsake its first love of Jesus Christ. God is looking for a woman, a church, who is willing to ascend the hill of prayer and desperately hang on to His word to return life to the house.

Immediately the woman knew her son was dead, she didn't give her husband an opportunity to organise burial arrangements but she laid her son on the prophet's bed. She knew that once she had placed him on the bed, he would then only be sleeping.

Most times when visions seem to be failing, we forget how we conceived them, and focus our eyes on the words and reactions of people.

The bed represents the will of God. It also represents the grave of Jesus Christ. It was necessary for Jesus to die and be laid in the grave for the church to overcome death and sin. His death gave us a second life that was full of victory and purity enabling us to stand before God.

To be able to accomplish great works of God, we need to lay our wills on the bed of Jesus so that he may raise us up with His life to preserve our dreams and bring them to life.

Romans 6:8-10

Now if we died with Christ, we believe that we shall also live with Him,

Knowing that Christ, having been raised from the dead, dies no more. Death no longer has dominion over Him. For the death that He died, He died to sin once for all, but the life that He lives, He lives to God.

When the woman reached the man of God, she used his own word to challenge him. She said, "Did I ask you to give me a son? Why did you lie to me?"

When I see people losing the love of God because He hasn't done what He promised them, they do not progress in the ministry, yet God called them. I just can't imagine their end. God who calls us, knows how, when and where He will use us.

If your dream seems like it's going to die, just give it back to the One who gave it to you. You didn't ask God to give your dream but He gave it to you with a purpose.

# CHAPTER EIGHT
# GOD COMES AT LAST

The later glory shall be greater than the former. The devil tried to exaggerate the situation but when the son started to work, the wedding became fabulous. People started from where they thought they had ended, there was abundance and overflow. I am here to say that it's not yet over with you. God is about to do a new thing in His church.

When everyone tasted the wine, they wondered where it had been kept for it was so fresh and tasted beautiful. The world says the longer the wine stays, the tastier it becomes, but with God He provides fresh wine every day as He did with the manna in the wilderness.

God doesn't want us to rely on the past but He wants us to seek his new grace every day. He says, 'renew your mind in the word of God'.

The wine tasted better because it was made from the water poured in the pots that were put aside for the purpose of sanctification according to the Jewish custom. The water was for the wedding guests to wash themselves before they feasted.

You will never get something new if you don't let go of the old, but you can use the old to get something new and better.

We are having a lot of contradictions in the church because some people are still hanging on to the doctrine that was taught in the seventies. Whenever God sends his word, it is for a particular purpose in a set time. So if we still live in the past message of the gospel, the old manna that means we are still living in the seventies even though we are in the twenty first century.

Not wanting to flow with the flow makes us become stumbling blocks, opposed against the move of God. God wants the wine to flow but all blockages must be attended to first.

I tell you, when the son of a woman starts to work, holding on to our old movements is going to stop. Everyone will want to taste the new wine because it's going to be different from all other wines. It's a wine that has been made out of purity.

When God began to move in Budadiri East, even the traditional churches, the Catholic and Church of England, who were so staid in their doctrines, felt the move of God. He moved in their churches until their way of worship changed and they began to worship like us. If they would not change, they would lose members.

God invaded them and they began praying until they started to speak in tongues, prophesy and be slain in the power of God. They began getting prophecies telling them to join the move of God that had started.

We have seen God raise for Himself mighty men and women from the traditional churches and they come to our churches to minister. God wants to do the same with his people everywhere in the world.

Start to pray that God will use you for this cause by giving you a beautiful beginning. The Bible says we are vessels in the house of God. It also says, out of our bellies shall flow the rivers of living water. God will only change our water into wine if we sanctify ourselves as God's vessels that are put aside for His glory.

The time of the vessels that carry processed wine is over because their wine was insufficient for everyone. Jesus couldn't afford to put new wine in the old wineskin, because He knew that they had years keeping processed wine. Therefore, the wine skins could rupture and destroy the new wine. Jesus warns us to put off the old wineskin if we are going to carry his glory.

God asks that His house be rebuilt before He brings the latter glory. Many have tried to carry God's glory and polluted it because they were not ready to change. No one can stand in the glory of God. If we try to stand in His glory without being ready we will fall.

Whenever God wanted to talk to the children of Israel, He would tell Moses to ask them to wash and sanctify themselves for three days before He would come.

Every time God came down, He would confirm His covenant that He made with their fathers, Abraham, Isaac and Jacob. He would continue to strengthen them that He would always be with them and protect them until they settled in the land He promised to their forefathers.

God doesn't want to come down to hassle or threaten us. He wants to have fellowship with us as his friends.

I believe in rebuking prophecies because if God longs for us to be His friends and then we subsequently refuse the offer, He turns against us. He is a consuming fire. God's desire is to be sending us friendly prophecies.

Haggai 2:
We see that as soon as they started doing what God had asked them to do, God's words turned to being positive and compassionate. He started to promise them greater things than what He had said before. He promised to help them finish the temple and to be with them always.

As pastors in Uganda allowed to laying down of all programs to follow the direction of God, He poured His favour upon the church. When there is a need to build a church, then a request goes out to the people to contribute. The response becomes enormous. Business people and even government officials come too, asking if they can contribute.

One time we were having a pastors' prayer meeting in one of the churches. One of our pastors stood up and requested that we pray for her to build a church. That very moment we felt led by God to make pledges. What was meant to be a prayer request became a dream come true. Others paid cash. This, together with the pledges, raised enough money to buy the land.

The pastors alone bought the land but when we went back to our churches and encouraged believers, we were able to raise enough money and materials to build the church. We have achieved so much as a result of working together.

When we organise our public meetings and go to the police to send us some officers to be present, more especially when we are having night meetings, the police honour our request, but before, one man would find it hard to approach them. Police work is to keep law and order so when they see an organised body they support with their full cooperation.

One night, all the churches had gathered on the ground during New Year's Eve prayers. We were busy praying, shouting and worshipping our God. When I turned around, our local MP had joined and he was down on his knees praying hard. After we finished praying and recognised his presence, he said he didn't come in the name of political representation but as he was driving home, the Holy Spirit spoke to him to come for prayers.

Every knee shall bow and every tongue confess that Jesus is Lord. We asked him to lead us in prayer for our land that night and he also promised that if we wanted any support in running the meetings, we should always contact him. God wants government officials to be involved in His move.

## When the Latter Gory is Present Even Our Governments Will Turn Back to God

Haggai 2:23
In that day, says the Lord of hosts, I will take you, Zerubbabel my servant, the son of Shealtiel, says the Lord and will make you like a signet ring. For I have chosen you, says the Lord of Hosts.

## Signet Ring

A signet ring is a seal of approval worn around necks, arms or a finger, as a sign of people's noble status. In the book of Esther we see that everyone the king gave his signet ring to, meant that he was acknowledged by the king and was to be given the same power as him.

We saw the seven were happy to see the plumbline in the hands of Zerubbabel even though the beginning was small. After Zerubbabel carefully and faithfully finished the house of God as he were instructed, God rewarded him by making him a signet ring between God and His people the Israelites. God transferred all His authority and power to Zerubbabel in order that he could govern God's people in the ways of God.

There is a special grace that comes upon a nation when its leaders turn back to God because there are some things that God can only use them to do that pastors can't.

Government leaders are the ones that work for the signet rings so that they may rebuild and bring peace and prosperity in the nation. Our leaders are targeted by either God or enemy. The responsibility of the church is to pray for the nation and the leaders to lead it in the ways of God.

I have seen many Christians say it is hard for government leaders to serve God and so they don't want to be involved in politics. Christians have limited their vision to everyone wanting to become pastors of churches. We have walked away from other major responsibilities.

As Christians gave up other professions to become pastors in the past, the enemy gained ground by putting his followers in leadership making it difficult for them to do the will of God.

When our leaders don't acknowledge God in their offices and lives, the nation misses that blessing God gives to the nations that fear Him.

Matt 28:18, 19
And Jesus came and spoke to them saying, all authority has been given to me in heaven and on earth. Go therefore and make disciples of all nations, baptizing them in the name of the Father and of the Son and of the Holy Spirit.

God is looking for the glorious house He can dwell in to destroy the invisible evil kingdoms that are influential in our communities. We have all heard about the history of Idi Amin.

Uganda is a small nation that was ripped apart by wars, famines and diseases like HIV aids, which claimed many lives.

Uganda once had the highest rate of HIV aids in the whole of Africa and probably the whole world.

We saw more than five members die in one family every day due to aids. It was rare to walk past two homes without seeing aids victims who were very ill. Death and grief covered the whole land.

One district was named after skulls even up to today because so many families died until there was no one left to bury each other. If you went to that community, you could find skeletons lying in the houses everywhere.

Uganda became a very hopeless nation with very many orphans. It was because of this, that organisations like Watoto and many others were formed.

# CHAPTER NINE
# IDI AMIN STARVED PEOPLE

I remember as a little girl, life was so hard that people were ordered to be in bed by 5:00 pm. When a patrol of soldiers passed and would find a home with electricity or candles still on or even hear a child crying, they would come and beat everyone in the house, then take away the man to be tortured or killed as a punishment for not looking after his family.

There were no basic provisions like sugar, salt or soap, People had to use natural salt from caves that animals had urinated on. They had to use certain tree leaves for washing and showers. They also drank coffee without sugar or add salt to enhance the taste. The only time they could access sugar was when it had been smuggled in from Kenya by someone risking his life. And when sugar was brought in, the word would secretly spread around, each neighbour telling others up to the last one. They would tell each other were they would meet to have at least a quarter of a kilo to take home.

I remember one day the news was leaked to Amin's soldiers about the sugar business and the people involved. When they arrived, they rounded up all the suspects and tied them on the back of their land rovers and dragged them alive along the road. They then tied them on trees, their heads facing down to show others the punishment for finding someone smuggling. They kicked them and used their guns to beat them in their faces. Every part of their body was full of blood, even in their ears.

During Amin's time many Christians were asked to give up their faith and become Muslims or die, as I told you before. Friday became the holy day and if any church was found praying on Sunday, all people in it would be killed.

So following all that had happened to Uganda as I have detailed, there arose a great revival in the 1990's and it swept the whole nation. Uganda felt the move of God in every area including the state house and the parliament.

One time there was a national prayer meeting going on which had gathered people from all over the nation. While the meeting was going on, the current president of Uganda appeared with heavily armed body guards. We all thought, 'what was the current president going to do?' When they acknowledged him and requested him to give a speech, he said these words, "For a very long time Uganda was ruled and protected by guns. Now as the president of Uganda, representing the nation of Uganda, I give this flag back to God, the nation of Uganda and her people will be led by God Himself."

From that day the grace and the favour of God came upon the nation so powerfully that the people began to prosper. We also saw God's protection, in that, whoever planned to attack our nation would be discovered and arrested.

Isaiah 9:2

The people who walked in darkness have seen a great light. Those who dwelt in the land of the shadow of death, upon them a light has shone.

## The Glory Can't Be Contained In One Place

The move of God in Budadiri East began to spread like wildfire until it has now engulfed the whole district of Sironko and the neighbouring regions. Pastors get invitations from some parts of Uganda asking them to go and impart the same move of God in their churches. When the glory comes and people try to contain it in one place, it causes tribulations and persecutions, but when people move, whenever they go, the revival spreads.

God wants His glory to spread like wild fire in the forest. When the forest catches on fire, all the animals, plants and everything in it burns. After everything is burned down, after sometime the trees which formerly had life grow again.

When the glory of God moves, everything in us dies, then we see the new Christ character in us.

# CHAPTER TEN
# THE LATTER GLORY FROM THE EAST

Matthew 2:2
Saying, where is He who has been born King of the Jews? For we have seen his star in the east and have come to worship him.

One time I was walking down a street in Kampala when God opened my eyes. I saw cars driving on a very rough, dusty, road with potholes everywhere through the bush and were travelling fast with very bright head lights. Regardless of the conditions of the road, the cars appeared to be going on a very smooth road.

After the vision I heard a voice say to me, "As you saw the sun rising in the east and moving in a westerly direction, so shall My glory be from the east to the west. Although My people will negotiate some wild and strange conditions, because of the brightness of My glory on them, they will pass through without realising negative circumstances. The people who will carry My glory are those ones with resilient spirits".

For many years I have wondered why God said His glory will start in the east.

Ezekiel 43:2
And behold the glory of the God of Israel came from the way of the east. His voice was like the sound of many waters; and the earth shone with his glory.

With Biblical proof of so many things that begun in the east, I have believed that the east is the starting point of God's moving. It's where the dawning of the new day starts. It is a place of fresh beginnings. The people who live in the east wake up every morning seeing the sun rising upon their heads and that gives them new hope for a new day even though they had had a bad night. Mourning and sorrow may endure in the night but joy comes in the morning.

Easterners never sleep but they stay awake and are watchful, their mind is sober as is their nature to start new things. Easterners don't sit comfortably in other people's histories but they themselves want to be the history makers. They want to have fresh plans and they also want to set beautiful beginnings in their lives and in the lives of others.

Jesus was born in the west of the city and the westerners had all the opportunities to cherish the Son but instead took Him for granted. They were already developed and established in the capital city that could attract people from all over the world. Their economy and political system controlled the world. People had to travel from every direction to register in the census.

At the time Jesus was born, people were busy doing things that were making themselves comfortable. They were busy doing things to make the World a one world order. They were busy creating laws to control people.

Mary and Joseph walked through the city gates and through the streets until they found the corral, no one was able to discern. I want to tell you that it's hard for people who live in the west to sense God's visitation because they don't easily open their doors to visitors. They only open them for those who have the same standards.

It was at night, after everyone had had a busy day sleeping, and others partying that Mary gave birth. We are aware of the 10 virgins: five were counted wise because they left their lamps burning and had extra oil and five were stupid because their lights went out due to a lack of oil. When the bridegroom arrived, they tried to go out and buy oil, but by the time they came back the door was closed.

As soon as Jesus was born his star appeared to the wise men, who were awake, sober the whole night. He told them about the good news of the King born in Israel and he instructed them to follow the star and worship Him.

You may challenge me to prove that the wise men were awake at night. Stars only appear at night after darkness covers the world and can be seen when you are standing outside in open space and lift your head up. There are so many stars in the sky but for these men to be able to make a distinction between stars, they were awake spiritually.

Here I am seeing the power of prayer. Every time we pray, we become refreshed, sober and awake, knowing the signs about the move of God that others don't know.

1 Thessalonians 5:4-7

But you, brethren, are not in darkness, so that this Day should overtake you as a thief.

You are all sons of light and sons of the day. We are not of the night nor of darkness.

Therefore let us not sleep, as others do, but let us watch and be sober.

For those who sleep, sleep at night, and those who get drunk are drunk at night.

In real life the wise men were wealthy and of royal blood. They could not have gone to see Herod if they were not of his same class of society. When the star appeared to them, the precious gifts they carried, they presented to Jesus in worship. Spiritually, the men were the wealthy of the wealthy because of the word in them. There is no greater wealth than God's word. God is looking for the royal priesthood who have got everything, to worship Him in truth and Spirit, while spiritual poverty strikes the world.

When a talent is hidden in you, it is called a treasure. But worse, when it's discovered, it becomes a gift. God wants us to open our treasures through prayer and use our gits to worship Him in Spirit and truth.

## The characteristics of the people from East:

They fast and pray for God to give them the message that will bring spiritual insight everywhere they go. They also ask God to show them the revelations that are sealed from the rest of the world. I hear the experts and the governments of this world have spent billions of dollars trying to find where the Ark of the Covenant was hidden. We should know that it was hidden by Jeremiah who was led by the Spirit of God to do so, therefore it will take someone or some people led by the same Spirit to find it for the glory of God.

2. They never get cold as they make themselves warm by setting fires to keep burning. In the night, while everyone else had covered themselves in beds, the three wise men were gathered around the fire. God wants us to have altars of fire in our hearts, and having them there, we will be able to do great things without being pushed to do them. The altar fills us with the zeal of God to be on fire for Christ. People who are consumed with zeal are not tossed by contrary winds nor offer lame excuses. Jesus warns in Matthew 24:12 that because lawlessness will abound, the love of many will grow cold. Revelation 3:so then, because you are lukewarm, and neither cold nor hot will I vomit you from My mouth. Those consumed with the zeal of fire will carry the government of God upon their shoulders.

3. Easterners are naturally singers and worshippers. When things go bad or they are lonely without no one to talk to, they create music. David became a worshipper because he used to sing while tending his father's flock. They are creative too. So the Angel told the men to go and worship because they were worshippers.

God is calling his church to be positioned in the east spiritually, whether you are geographically from the west, east, north or south. He wants His church to be ready and waiting, not sleeping. He says those who wait upon the Lord shall renew their strength. If you wait on the Lord, even if you live in the west (the place of abundance), you won't become complacent.

God has raised many people from humble beginnings but as soon as they move to the west, a place of comfort, they forget Him. They feel like they have arrived, that they have got everything, so there is no need to seek and wait on God. God has brought people to the west to show them His abundance, but this abundance is never meant to replace Him. Even in abundance, we are to remain faithful and totally dependent on Him, as in former times.

Revelation 3:14-18
Because you say, "I am rich, have become wealthy, and have need of nothing – and do not know that you are wretched, miserable, poor, blind, and naked. I counsel you to buy from me – gold refined in the fire that you may be clothed, that the shame of your nakedness may not be revealed; and anoint your eyes with eye salve, that you may see.

## Donkeys and Horses

> Tell the daughter of Zion,
> Behold, your King is coming to you,
> Lowly, and sitting on a donkey,
> A colt, the foal of a donkey.    Mathew 21:5

Normally, whenever there is talk of a king or any leader of a nation coming to the city, they are expected to arrive in heavily guarded helicopters or specially made armoured cars. When the entourage passes, everyone knows they are passing according to the security restrictions and uniqueness of their cars.

The nation of Israel had been waiting for King Jesus to come for a long time. The fact was that everyone was excited at His expected coming. But they didn't know how, when and where. They were comparing His coming to the same standards of the earthly kings

During those days, if the king was being driven through the city, he would be on the best and highest bred horse chariots. Only wealthy people could afford to own horses, but the poor could only afford donkeys.

Mary, who carried King Jesus in her womb, and while on the donkey, no one paid attention, the people only saw these poor, struggling couple from the countryside. Thank God that they came in a humble way. If they had come on horses, Herod would have sought to kill them and stop Jesus from being born. They might have also scared people into running away thinking they were Roman soldiers coming to cause chaos in the city.

When the revival is about to be birthed, it comes in humility that is inconspicuous, mild, gentle and meek. It comes with greater power than the armed and mighty military; it comes in the power of humble wisdom and penetrating love. Meekness is not weakness, but power under perfect control.

We have seen people in the past who claimed to have brought revivals in cities. Before they come, they wanted curtain standards to be met and if one or two things were missing, they wouldn't be ashamed to cancel the meetings. They wouldn't care about the lost souls they were concerned of keeping their reputation and wanted to do things to impress people.

Jesus chose the donkey among all animals to carry Him because it's a very simple animal that can carry heavy weights on its back without getting tired or complaining. In fact, if a donkey is given underweight luggage to carry, it refuses to move and lies down until more weight is added!

Poor people don't use donkeys for pleasure but they use them to earn a living or for survival.

When you look at its back, it has a cross that divides its back into four parts. That cross is believed to be the cross of Jesus.

Jesus said whoever is worthy to be His disciple should carry his cross and follow Him. Once God's glory is revealed in us, it becomes so intense, so heavy for us to carry in our own strength. So what it does is lower us down so that God himself may lift us in humility, willingness and gentleness to be able to sustain His glory.

God is looking for servants with a donkey's heart to usher in His glory to the world, people who are willing to carry what they have been given without complaining. It doesn't matter where you are and what you look like, even if you are still bound, as long as you lower yourself and take on the characteristics of a donkey. God is going to send for you to come and usher in His glory in high places.

# CHAPTER ELEVEN
# THE COST AND THE CHALLENGES

Matthew 10:38-39
And he who does not take his cross and follow after me is not worthy of me. He who finds his life will lose it and he who loses his life for my sake will find it.

The cross has no meaning to us if the precious life of the Son of God was not sacrificed on it. In fact, the original purpose of the cross was a place of horror and death. I want to explain to you how you can change your place of horror into a place of praise. Jesus has never asked us to leave our crosses behind, He simply wants us to carry them and follow him. I hope this message finds a place in someone's life who is wandering in the valley of dry bones.

There is a saying that there is only one life in this life. Once you have run your course you can't live your life over again. But Christ says, "You have to lose your life in order to find it." We all treasure our lives and our individual moments. We are concerned when anything wrongs us or things we don't want happen to us. Christ wants us to carry our crosses and follow him, just as He carried His cross and followed His father. He doesn't encourage us to follow Him empty handed.

I have seen people who have failed to reach their goals because they wanted to solve their problems first. They were too frightened to walk on the path of life. What about the man who leaves his daughter who is dying and runs to look for Jesus. Didn't he love and adore his little girl like any daddy would do?

The people who don't want to take steps of faith are like a child who wants to walk but is too frightened to stand up. The mother, who knows that it is time for her baby to walk is going to force it to walk on the edge. Even if this is too upsetting for the child, at least the child gains the confidence to walk.

What are your concerns? Are they too hard for God to handle? Most times we offer excuses that lead us in not fulfilling the purpose of God for our lives. And if God's purpose is not realised in us, He will always find someone else willing to take the double portion which you have forsaken through disobedience.

Matthew 11:28-30
Come to me, all of you who labour and are heavy laden and I will give you rest. Take my yoke upon you and learn from me, for I am gentle and lowly in heart, and you will find rest for your souls. For my yoke is easy and my burden is light.

Our pastors did it hard sometimes for the sake of the kingdom. Have you ever been in situations where you feel God is telling you to do something but your personal desires also rise? Our pastors didn't have a stable source of income, when God called them. They totally had to rely on Him not worry about their problems. Some of them had families to look after and education for their children, etc. Sometimes they would walk for kilometres under the burning, hot sun to pastor churches or preach the gospel of Christ.

There is a situation where some people come to church hoping that it is the place where their problems can be solved so they expect the pastors to look after them. They come when they are broken hearted with sick children who need medical attention and can't afford to pay for it. Some come when they are hungry and have been starving for days with their children without anything to eat. They expect the pastors to look after them.

Isaiah 58:6-7
Is this not the fast that I have chosen: to lose the bonds of wickedness, to undo the heavy burdens, to let the oppressed go free, and that you break every yoke? Is it not to share your bread with the hungry, and that you bring to your house the poor who are cast out; when you see the naked, that you cover him and not hide yourself from your own flesh.

Because there is unity in the place, the pastors who can afford support in their churches help other pastors who can't, but they can't do it all.

I am so grateful to God that our pastors try as much as they can to help one another. They have learned to share one another's burdens. Because of this God is continuously giving them favour and blessing them.

My idea in writing this book was that it might be a two-way blessing. While you get blessed by reading the inspirational messages and stories of what God has done, your money goes to helping the pastors. God put this burden on our hearts. My husband and I support the pastors as they continue to fulfil what God has called them to do. We started doing this with our small income irrespective of our own bills and financial commitments. As the need increased, we realised that we could no longer do this on our own. So we prayed and asked God to open ways and this is when He led us to write this book based on what God did in the pastors, through the pastors and for the pastors.

# CHAPTER TWELVE

# THE VISION FOR THE BUDADIRI EAST PASTORS

Matthew 13:44
Again, the kingdom of heaven is like a treasure hidden in a field, which a man found and hid; and for joy over it he goes and sells all that he has and buys that field.

After the servants of God had put aside all their plans, and having sought the face of God together, they finally came up with a grand vision for the community that was above their small personal visions they had before. They also realised that God had given them the same goals, strategies and dreams, to see them affect the community to build a strong body of Christ first. They also sought the Lord to show them everyone's area of participation in the vision they had acquired. Having done all that, they are now working industriously toward the realisation of that vision.

For a very long time, God has been speaking to His church to be positioned for the outpouring of His blessing. But the church has failed to understand or to ask God which way He wants them positioned. The blessing God wants to pour out will not only be enough for His children but He wants it to influence and flood our cities, villages and communities. We all have to be willing to give up our personal interests and follow after God's treasures. He says 'seek ye first the kingdom of God and all these things shall follow you.'

The Bible talks of a rich young man who wanted to follow Jesus but he wasn't willing to go back and sell all his belongings for Jesus' sake. We can't follow Jesus while we are bowed down with our rich mentality. He wants us to invest our riches in Him, in order to possess the kingdom of God. He has never called us to just have the knowledge of His kingdom but He has given us the opportunity to buy and own it forever. Without submission to His will, we will just know about Kingdom wealth but fail to enjoy it.

The pastors, having realised the greatness of working together, surrendered all their desires at the feet of Jesus and He, Himself became the master planner of the overall project. Now, when they stand to share the vision, you find yourself being touched with the desire to become part of it. Whenever any of them go anywhere for ministry and get blessed, they bring some of the money and put it toward the vision's building treasury.

They now plan to have a good hospital, university and other programs. They also dream of turning their villages into one vibrant city. This giant dream came as a result of realising that when many dreams come together, they can produce great results.

God has promised to raise us from dust to glory. He has also promised that those who know Him to do great things. To know God is to follow him and do what He says. Once God establishes these things through these humble servants, the community cannot fail to see the kingdom of God being established.

God wants to show His glory through His church. He wants to display great works beyond the basic and ordinary things that any man can do. Imagine what would happen in the nations, if the body of Christ becomes one and starts doing things together. We will see nations transformed and God will give back the things that were formerly taken by the enemy.

The enemy fights to see that God's people will never come up with one dream and purpose in Jesus Christ. He wants everyone do his own thing so that he can weaken the army of Christ so they become powerless.

## Ezekiel's Ministry and Deeper Insight

Ezekiel 47:1Then he brought me back to the door of the temple; and there was water flowing from under the threshold of the temple toward the east, for the front of the temple faced east; the water was flowing from under the right side of the temple, south of the altar. (You can read the whole chapter.)

Ezekiel was a major prophet whom God had used, and was shown great things in his days. He had stood before great kings to warn them to turn to God. At one point, he was led by the Spirit of God to the valley of dry bones to speak life to them so they might live again.

Chapter 47 of Ezekiel is the second last chapter, which means he was about to come to the end of his ministry and probably retire. Let's assume, he had started to look back and count his achievements in ministry.

But it was at that very moment a man takes him back to the door of the temple and opens his eyes to see the water flowing from under the threshold of the temple. It seems that in all his life time in ministry, he had never had a personal encounter with God apart from being used by God.

You see there is a difference between having success in serving Jesus and knowing what He means to your life. The Bible clearly tells us that Jesus is the living water that will flow out of us if we only believe in Him.

John 7:38, John 4: 14.
But whoever drinks of this water that I shall give him will never thirst again. But the water that I shall give will become in him a fountain of water springing up into everlasting life.

Jesus was therefore this hidden water that Ezekiel saw, when he turned back to the door. This process of turning back to the door is called revival, restoration, reformation or refilling. The temple represents the presence of God. He was taken to the door to see the river Jesus that flows from God's presence and then walk through it.

It was necessary for Ezekiel to be filled with Jesus first in order to see the secret revelations of God.

After being revived, he then saw the water flowing towards the east and from the right side of the temple, south of the altar. Jesus is sitting at the right hand of the Father. Even though He is a King and Son of God, when it comes to pleading for our cause, He places Himself in a position of humility at the south side for God to forget all our past to start a fresh work in us.

East represents freshness or the beginning of God's moving. Jesus has put Himself low before God by humbling himself on our behalf so that through Him, we may be positioned in the East.

Also, east is where God revealed his great news to the wise men. People who live in the East have to be low and humble before Christ just as Christ is to God.

When you continue reading Ezekiel 47, you find that after Ezekiel saw the water, God began doing a new work in him. Before, he was getting messages about others, but his own life was dry and he needed an encounter with God's presence.

The man knew how much Ezekiel needed this water. As soon as Ezekiel arrived, he lowered his eyes to the south and humbled himself to receive from God. He was able to see the water on the altar's south side.

The Bible tells us to humble ourselves under the mighty hand of God so that He may raise us up in due time. If we learn to look southwards in God's presence, (that is, lowering ourselves to the ground as to appear as nothing), He will give us fresh ideas, fresh revelations and fresh anointing for His glory.

When we look to the North by neglecting the man's directive, we will miss out on God's visitation. We will find ourselves doing things very differently from what the Spirit of God maybe doing at that hour. This is when we will realise that God has sent his angel in the form of a man, but it will be too late.

In prior times Ezekiel was being used as a vessel. But after walking through the water, He found God's favour to become His child.

John 1:12
But as many as received Him, to them He gave the right to become children of God, to those who believed in His name.

As we continue to read I want us to ask ourselves, in which capacity are we serving God. Are we serving as vessels, servants, friends or children? I will explain my understanding about each of these later, so that you can decide for yourself.

Every time we walk through the river Jesus, our lives get cleansed and perfected to be worthy to see the unsearchable things stored ahead of us. There are some things we are not going to access unless we get the password of revival.

**A Vessel:** In acts 9 from verse 10, you see that Paul was being used as a vessel, even when the Lord sent Ananias to go and pray for him. Ananias found he had to go to Paul who was known for persecuting the Church of Christ. But in verse 15: Jesus replies to Ananias: "Go, for he is My chosen vessel to bear My name before gentiles, kings, and the children of Israel.

A vessel has no choice but to carry whatever has been put in it. It can be used to carry good or bad things. Saul was chosen by God to serve, but because he was just a vessel the enemy had gotten hold of him to stand against God. All he needed to fulfil God's purpose was to change from Saul, a multipurpose name, to Paul, a name chosen by God for His purpose alone.

The characteristic of the people serving God under the influence of the name Saul are: when we serve God as vessels, sometimes we find ourselves persecuting the work of God unknowingly. Being vessels can limit us by setting up boundaries and focusing on our small denominations rather than the wider plan of Jesus Christ.

Most times, when we introduce ourselves to other people as Christians, and when someone asks about our place of fellowship and finds out that we are not of the same denomination, they don't want anything to do with us. When such people don't want to integrate as children of God, I see them as vessels.

**A Servant:** trembles before their master and some servants don't necessarily get paid for their labour. Those that God calls tremble and fall at His feet. When we hear the voice of God, we cannot remain standing. When the Lord called Saul, he fell down. We also see many other occasions in the Bible, when people would fall on their faces whenever they heard the voice of God. Falling at God's presence is a sign of acknowledging His Lordship and your willingness to follow and do anything He would require from you. However, a servant can be willing but may not know his master's secrets. Some servants do recognise Jesus' Lordship but are not sensitive to the times and the moving of the Holy Spirit. In most cases, because they don't receive His revelation, they want things to be done their way not the Holy Spirit's way. They don't get the revelation because they don't have time to seek Him.

John 15:14-15
You are my friends if you do whatever I command you.

No longer do I call you servants, for a servant does not know what his master is doing; but I have called you friends, for all things that I heard from the father I have made known to you.

**A Friend:** Everyone wants a good friend but the relationship develops only after testing the patience and the humility in one another. Jesus called his servants friends after they had been obedient to His word. To be promoted from servant-hood to friendship requires a great deal of trust, and trust is developed over a period of time. A friend can be trusted to look after the master's business but he cannot inherit it and has less privileges.

**A child:** is an heir to His father's inheritance. He is bone of his bone and flesh of his flesh. A child has the father's similarities and takes full responsibility of the father's business with a heart of ownership.

John 16:15
All the things that the Father has are mine. Therefore I said that He will take of mine and declare it to you.

Many times when I am invited to minister in other churches, the first thing I look for before serving is, "I am working in my Father's house". My heart's desire is to make the house of God into what He wants it to be. I don't look to the leader of the ministry and to what I should receive for my service.

We have got to stop thinking in our little boxes and look at the wider perspectives if truly we are children of God.

Jesus never built the temple but when He walked into it and found those who were believed to be the leaders, using it to do other things other than the will of His Father, He was consumed with the will of His Father and began to turn the tables upside down, disorganising the businesses that were being conducted in the house of God. He Said, "My Father's house is not a house of thieves but it's a house of prayer". The sense of leadership activated Him to reclaim the true purpose of his Father's house.

God is looking for His children who will be bold enough to put His church in order. There has been a lot of ungodly business going on, under His cover, yet there is no display of His righteousness. God is looking for His children to establish His image in the church without walls.

When Jesus came, He found we were just vessels of the enemy. Through His love, He bought us to be His servants. And when we obeyed the criteria of servant-hood, He trusted us to become His friends.

Now He wants us to become children so that we may lead in that which belongs to the kingdom of his Father. Never be content with the first stage. Jesus wants to take us to higher places if we will continue walking with Him.

Friends could not become children until He died. His blood made us flesh of His flesh and bone of His bones, through accepting him as our personal Lord and Saviour.

In the book of Revelation, after He had given us the right to become children through His death, He made us to be kings with Him.

Revelation 1:5-6
And from Jesus Christ the faithful witness, the first born from the dead, and the ruler from all the kings of the earth. To Him who loved us and washed us from our sins in His blood, and has made us kings and priests to His God and Father, to Him be the glory and dominion forever and ever. Amen.

Our God has not only called us to study about his kingdom, He wants us to be heirs to the throne and enjoy his kingdom benefits here on earth.

God began taking Ezekiel on His water fulfilling journey. He says there is no condemnation to those who are in Christ Jesus.

Ezekiel had served God as a prophet but for the rest of his life God wanted him to be lost in Him, to be filled in the water, Jesus Christ. He began filling him from the legs until he could no longer cross the river. God's plan is to bring us into the overflow of His kingdom. Jesus' passion is about establishing a kingdom that has no walls or traditions, a kingdom where every knee will bow down and confess that He is Lord in worship and adoration.

Matthew 6:9-10.
In this manner, therefore, pray: Our Father in heaven, hallowed be your name. Your kingdom come. Your will be done on earth as it is in heaven.

Finally, Ezekiel was returned to the bank of the river and he noticed many trees that carried life for all living creatures.

In Genesis, man was driven out of God's presence for eating from the forbidden tree. But in Ezekiel's case, he got to discover the divine healing and provision that was present in the trees, by being led through the river Jesus.

Adam disobeyed God by eating the tree of the knowledge of good and evil, whereas Ezekiel is discovering the trees of healing and life through his obedience in following God's direction. When you obey, you eat the fruit of the land.

I believe if Ezekiel was today's man of God, he would have challenged the man by the great knowledge he had of the Bible. He would have asked the man about his ministry experience first.

This is exactly how most men and women of God have missed God's visitation. They think they know everything and even to the extent of how God should work. God has always sent genuine angels to churches but they haven't always been received because of the way they appeared, talked, or because of their background. The Holy Spirit finds it hard to penetrate a church that depends on their knowledge.

I will tell you the difference between a "Holy Spirit church" and a "church that depends on their own knowledge" later. Thank God for all the achievements but it is time to forsake all those achievements and get back to the plan of God.

Jesus left the church to build His kingdom not individual churches. When I see people struggling to build churches, I wish they would understand the revelation that Jesus has already built His church on the rock and no gates of hell shall prevail against it.

If they could only know that on the cross Jesus said, 'It is finished'. Then they would be enjoying the goodness of salvation and the benefits of being in God's presence.

When we all get the secret of building the kingdom, then the church of Christ will be able to rule in this world in victory and glory.

We are struggling and taking a lot of time to accomplish small things. God has a giant dream waiting for us to be a part of. God wants to show us great and unsearchable things just as he showed his servant Ezekiel.

# The Difference between a Holy Spirit Led Church and a Church That Depends on Their Knowledge

I have no problem with either church, but the reality is that a Spirit filled church is a place where you go and find people who are hungry and thirsty for God's word. You find people desperate for God's presence, never ceasing in seeking God's face in prayer.

They are willing to listen to anyone regardless and also they don't judge by sight. These people are passionate to do the things of God in love without anyone asking them to do so. In fact, with a burning fire inside them, they just seek any opportunity to do things rather than opportunities seeking them.

We have read similar experiences in the Bible where people were filled with the passion to give by the Spirit of God. After King Solomon prayed to God, the spirit of God stirred up people's hearts to give until Solomon asked them to stop.

We also see in the Acts of the Apostles that people gave until no one was in need. This is what we want to see in our churches. We give until there is no one in need amongst us. If you are a pastor of a church who struggles with people not giving, even if you prepare giving messages, you need the Spirit of God to take over your church.

We have seen people give the same day they give their lives to God yet they were never taught about giving. The Spirit of God just touches them to give because they are open to Him.

Finally, their leaders or pastors don't often preach from notes they were taught but spend time in the presence of God asking Him to give them the rhema word that is full of revelations that ministers to people's needs rather than consoling them. The Bible clearly tells us that wherever Jesus went He brought healing signs and wonders. Where are these things today? Isn't Jesus Christ the same yesterday, today and forever?

Isaiah 61:1
The spirit of the Lord God is upon me, because the Lord has anointed me to preach good tidings to the poor, He has sent me to heal the broken hearted, to proclaim liberty to the captives and the opening of the prison to those who are bound.

If you continue to read the whole of Isaiah 61, you will have a clear picture of the works of the Holy Spirit, how they manifest in a Spirit-led church.

In a church relying on knowledge, people don't take the word of God seriously and in most cases they use their knowledge to challenge the revelations of God. Before the pastor gives the word, they already know what he will talk about, because he gives them notes ahead of time.

Secondly, this type of leader has a yearly calendar that shows what is meant to be taught each Sunday. They don't believe in God sending someone with a message if it is not in line with their program, or they haven't gone through their ministry training programs for approval. In this set up, you find people who have become complacent about the things of God. The church then becomes a seminary or a historical place where people go just to get the knowledge of the past.

They also don't live by faith, but by sight. People don't want to give so are reminded every Sunday to give. People don't change because they are filled with the knowledge of men.

In this case people strive to maintain Christian values, when they have been robbed by the enemy of their Christian rights. They are not conscious of God and His direction but are worried about building their own doctrine to be seen by people.

God's simple word to Adam was, obey and stay in my garden of fullness, a garden that flows with gold and all the precious stones. But Adam thought that was not enough to make him a man and sought for knowledge. What did knowledge do? It turned him away from God's presence. It is a good thing to have God's knowledge but having knowledge without the revelation of the Holy Spirit is very dangerous.

In that case, you find people starting to fight and hinder the move of God instead of embracing it, like Simeon did. If we trust the Holy Spirit, He will show us great and unsearchable things. God is again calling His church from the place of knowing about Him to the place of wanting to know Him.

Our God searches our hearts and examines our thoughts. What was the motivation or driving force that caused you to want to know Him? He is calling us back to the starting point of wanting to know Him, for He already knows why we are there.

God is in the process of shaking the foundations to see which material the churches were built of.

Are they good or dangerous to His kingdom? He doesn't look at how high, magnificent and powerful the building may be but he is after a building that is built with His materials. It may look simple, but as long as it doesn't harm his saints, His bride, whom He went to prepare a place for. He doesn't want to come and find his people with chronic problems and injuries they received as a result of sheltering under dangerous buildings.

Pastors, men and women of God, we are the building that I am talking about. You have finally found your way to lead God's people. Check yourself first. Are you doing the right thing by God? Are you living an example to the people you lead? Is your character worth following? God is not after your service, gifts and anointing. He wants your heart. We are more worried about wanting to serve God's people rather than preparing ourselves first.

I have sat back and watched many people who call themselves servants of God. They rush into ministry with the objective of having a name. Everywhere they go they create strife and division. I want us to know that such people will never be friends of Jesus. He uses someone else to build His church and then because of greed they come and divide it. They don't care whether people kill one another or Christians get confused as long as they have their own way.

God doesn't send us to cause division but he sent us to bring unity, reconciliation and love. I have seen many preachers who have been invited to churches and have been warmly received with one heart but they break and start churches out of churches.

Normally the churches they start are with disobedient members; probably someone had committed adultery and is under discipline. When these preachers come, the first thing they see in these people is the heavy anointing and the call that God has put on them that the pastor was hindering. He didn't want him to serve God.

I have always carried these questions along with me. Which God is it who divides churches to establish an alternative church? Why does God give someone a too heavy anointing? God took our heavy burdens that we may carry His light one. I believe the heavy anointing that some people carry around is the anointing of the devil to divide, steal, kill and destroy. By their fruit, not gifts or anointing, you shall know them.

Therefore, whoever you may be in your calling, whenever you move around to tell people how many churches you have while promoting yourself, remember, every work is going to be tested or shaken. And if the work collapses, I want to assure you that the blood of all those people you misled will be upon your head.

You have taken people from being repentant of their sins to turning them into master rebels with ministry names. Just as a wolf cannot hide in a sheep skin, wherever you take these people, the heavy anointing you saw is going to manifest your true character. You may operate in this heavy anointing, but the issues that haven't been dealt with will destroy your testimony.

I tell you, no one would like his/her testimony to be destroyed while serving the Lord. When that happens, it takes long time to rebuild trust in people.

There is a proverb in my language, One day people were chasing a hyena that had eaten all the sheep in the village and they wanted to kill it. So whoever heard the cry joined in the hunt to kill it. But when it reached a particular place, he said to the hyena, "why are they pursuing you? Don't they know that you survive on blood? Come into my house and I will hide you. I will tell them that I haven't seen you, when they ask." So thankfully the hyena took refuge under his shelter while the whole village came running towards the place in the direction they saw the hyena go.

They asked him to join them and had he seen it? He said he was busy and never saw anything. So the men continued in the hunt until they finally thought the hyena was out of the village and returned to their homes.

Two days later, the hyena turned on his protector. The man said to the hyena, "no, you can't do that to me! Remember I saved you when all the men were searching to kill you."

The hyena said, "you know that I cannot live without blood, you even said that to me. At this point yours is the only blood I have to survive.' The hyena told him, "you would have been better off letting me die than living to see you". Then the hyena grabbed the man, mauled him and ate him. He then continued on his journey.

When the neighbours got up the next morning they noticed that the man had been eaten. They then realised that he was killed by the hyena and that he had been hiding it.

This is a great lesson to us pastors who think we can do better than others. When Christians come to us complaining of their former churches, instead of working together with the former pastors to solve the problems, we work against them in order to fill our pews.

Pastors have this thinking that people leave other churches to come to them because they are hurting. I tell you if someone came to you while hurting, there is no way you are going to heal that wound without knowing the cause.

You can only know the cause if you go to the place where he/she was wounded. Trying to heal a wound, in which you don't know the cause, will turn to cancer. That is why doctors, before they proceed on any operation, ask many questions.

A wounded soul will never speak wrong against himself/herself but will tell you how bad the other person was. A monkey will never vote for a forest to be cut down because that's its life.

If you are pastoring a church full of wounded people, every time you speak something you actually cause them more pain. That is why pastors are preaching diluted messages because they don't want to hurt people.

If they hurt them, they will end up running away to start other churches where people are counselled but are not treated for their ailments. I call it an HIV AIDS church. AIDS never gets cured but can be controlled. So it is in a church where people's problems and afflictions are controlled but not healed by God's word. And if an epidemic is controlled it becomes a carrier. We have so many controlled rebels in our churches who have become carriers of rebellion that influence new coverts whenever they go.

If you are the kind of a pastor who started a church because you thought you and some people were hurt, I want to boldly inform you that you have started a control centre. The word of God tells me that God's church is built on the foundation of apostles and prophets. If God has called us to heal the broken hearted and bind up their wounds, then it has to be in a church where they have been wounded.

If you are working as a mediator, ask God to give you wisdom on how to handle the situation between the wounded person and the one who wounded them.

Sometimes people come to me complaining of what their pastors did to them. I have always stood my ground, telling these people about their pastors' goodness and probably what caused the wounds.

Sometimes, if we are in a spirit-filled church, our pastors can be led to speak wounding words that bring healing. The Bible tells us that our God wounds and He heals. Why does He wound and then heal at the same time? Salvation, accepting Jesus takes seconds, but transformation is a process that requires time. The process takes the word of God that comes into our lives. It destroys, uproots, kills, dismantles and then it rebuilds, plants, raises, reforms, restores etc., as is seen in the call of Jeremiah.

In the actual process when a house is being destroyed, you see dust and stones rumbling against each other, but when it is rebuilt, you see it standing complete and very glorious. So some people want the glory of salvation (God), but they don't want the process of transformation. When the process is taking place, they feel uncomfortable and offended. So during the process of breaking down the character and other things that the enemy had built in us, is what the Bible calls God wounding us. And the time of rebuilding is when God heals us. The word of God is a double-edged sword. It cuts through and divides the heart. Doctors use sharp objects to operate, but the overall objective of healing is what matters. They don't cut to destroy but heal. That's why before Jacob became Israel, the angel of God had to wound him first. He was wounded to the point that he limped. The angel was not worried about the pain he was causing Jacob, but that he was not going to call him Israel until he admitted he was Jacob.

We see many people wanting to be called Israel, but they don't want to admit that they are Jacobs first. So when God starts to wrestle with them, they complain. The angel was determined to wrestle Jacob the whole night, even if Jacob was trying to hide his identity. He broke Jacob to the point where he saw that he no longer had the strength to fight the angel. That is when he finally asked his name. If Jacob had known and told the angel his name beforehand, he would have not gone through the dark or night of pain. Jacob wanted his name to change, which is why he struggled and wouldn't let the angel go until he blessed him. Did you know that most of us come to God because we want to be blessed, but we don't want to change from our wicked ways? However, God's condition is clear in 2 Chronicles 7:14

"If my people who are called by my name will humble themselves and pray and seek my face, and turn from their wicked ways, then I will hear from heaven and will forgive their sin and heal their land."

# CHAPTER THIRTEEN
# THE LAST PERSON

Mathew 20:16
So the last will be first and the first last, for many are called but few chosen.

There is a very significant meaning about the word last. It is reserved for the best outcome and our God comes at last. We saw at the wedding that Jesus performed a miracle of wine at last when they had run out of the first wine which wasn't enough for everyone. We also saw prophet Haggai promising that the glory of the latter house would be greater than the former. We also saw that after Jesse, David's father, brought in all his sons, Samuel asked for the last born who had not been considered. Probably Jesse didn't bother to call him because he thought that there was no way he would be chosen. He was the outcast of the family who was isolated in the bush looking after livestock because it was the only job his father had given him. Little did he know that God put him there to be trained for such a day when he would kill Goliath and bring great victory to Israel and also become a great king. As soon as Jesse mentioned of David's existence, Samuel put everything on hold and ordered everybody to remain standing until David arrived.

David became the first person to kill Goliath and caused the whole army of the philistines to flee. He was the first to become king in his father's house and the tribe of Judah.

Another example is about a young man in the Bible who another had hurried to bring the message to the king, but when the king lifted his eyes, he saw this young man coming down from the mountains on foot. The king didn't open any letter but he said, let's wait until the young man I see coming down the hills arrives and we hear what he has to say first. The king received the young man's massage and made a decision based on it rather than other. The young man's massage caused a great change for it was the massage everyone was waiting for.

The whole world is asking, who is that person who is going to bring revival? Where is the house that is going to display the latter glory and who is that person who going to finish the last leg in the race?

I want to encourage you that your race is not yet over and God has not forsaken you. You may be still struggling with practicing while others come to practice and then go to compete. You would rather fail many times while practicing than failing on the competition ground. Many people rush to win but they don't want to do the prior practice.

I want to encourage you in that you are still in the race and God has positioned you to take the last baton change. In real life the person who takes the last baton change has to be the fastest runner and people have confidence in him to win the race. I want to tell you that our God comes last because He is the best therefore He has positioned you in the last place because He knows you are the best.

You may be wondering why you have prayed and fasted yet nothing is happening. You have done everything the right way and still nothing is happening. Sometimes, when you see things are about to happen, that's when everything turns out differently. My friend, know that nothing else is holding you back other than God Himself for the appointed time. I want to encourage you that keep warming up in that position by reading the word of God and holding fast to His promises. Reach out to someone who is about to pass the baton to you. You are not only racing for yourself, but you are representing your nation, the kingdom of God. I can see a standstill in the kingdom, some things have been put on hold. There is a feast in the making waiting for the day of celebration. I see the heavenly band lining up with flutists and trumpets ready to blow for your win. I want to tell you that your victory is going to cause the Kingdom anthem to be sung and the flag to be raised high. The whole Kingdom is waiting for your win so be well assured that you will win because your training manager is the best.

## Not All "Last" Persons Win the Race what's Gone Wrong?

My dear, as you are on the line waiting for the baton to be passed to you, I want you to take precaution on these things. Most people fail to finish strong because they panic and lose confidence in themselves due to concentrating on grabbing the baton on time. The baton is the word of God. Some people, when they see others doing better than them, lose trust in the word and begin to believe in what the enemy might be doing. You find Christians washed by the blood of Jesus believing in what the enemy is doing more than trusting in the word of God.

They also start to cheat: it doesn't matter, whether you become number one, but once you cheat your position will be cancelled. You will be placed in the last place where even the last in the race gets a percentage and immediately you will be eliminated from the game. It's like the story of two hares and the elephant when they argued about a race to see who would win. The hares were identical. One was at the starting line and the other at the finishing post. They tricked the elephant to run faster and leave the hare behind but when the elephant reached the finishing post, the hare was already there. The elephant was left wondering how fast the hare was without even considering that there may be two of them.

God is not mocked. People have failed because of double mindedness. They think they can trick God. You may think you are tricking Him but in the end you will be the one to lose out on the great plans He had for you. Until we learn to stand still, we will never be able to see the glory of God. You have got the choice to choose the word of God or the negative words of the enemy that he tries to throw at you.

Don't be a vessel, but be a responsible child and a friend of God who holds His secrets and know what your Father is capable of doing.